San Francisco

p76
p79
p84
p87
p90

0   600 yds
0   600 m

San Francisco Bay

Alcatraz 2

Pier 45
USS Pampanito
Pier 39
Balclutha
Eureka
SF Maritime National Historic Park
Cannery
FISHERMAN'S WHARF
1
Aquarium of the Bay
The Embarcadero

Fort Mason Center
FORT MASON
SF National Maritime Museum
Ghirardelli Square
North Point Street

12

RUSSIAN HILL PARK

San Francisco Art Institute

TELEGRAPH HILL
Telegraph Hill
Colt Tower
Lewi's Plaza
N.E. Waterfront Historic District
EMBARCADERO

Columbus Ave

Lombard St

RUSSIAN HILL

NORTH BEACH

City Lights Bookstore

3

Ferry Building

Transamerica Pyramid

The Heart

Broadway

Haas-Lilienthal House

Cable-Car Museum

Bank of America

Washington St

Embarcadero

Whittier Mansion

Spreckels Mansion

LAFAYETTE PARK

Grace Cathedral

NOB HILL

Van Ness Ave

Franklin St

California St

Pine St

Masonic Center

7

CHINATOWN

Chinatown Gateway

4

Crocker Galleria

Pine St

FINANCIAL DISTRICT

California St

Hallidie Bldg

Pine St

UNION SQUARE

Museum of the African Diaspora

5

Cartoon Art Museum

San Francisco Museum of Modern Art

Japan Center

8

St Mary's Cathedral

Geary St

O'Farrell St

TENDERLOIN

Market St

i

YERBA BUENA GARDENS

Moscone Center

80

Expressway

Gough St

Old Mint

Zeum

Asian Art Museum

Orpheum Theater

MARKET

Harrison St

James Lick Skyway

City Hall

CIVIC CENTER PLAZA

6

SF Public Library

4th & King Station

HAYES VALLEY

Fulton St

Hayes St

Mission St

Market St

9th St

Phoenix Theater

Market St

The Center

Van Ness Ave

10th St

Bryant St

80

Southern Embarcadero Freeway

Central Skyway

James Lick Freeway

Potrero Avenue

280

16th St

Mission Dolores

11

Guerrero St

Dolores St

South Van Ness Avenue

16th St

17th Street

MISSION

MISSION DOLORES PARK

POTRERO

INSIGHT GUIDES

SAN FRANCISCO

Step by Step

APA PUBLICATIONS L

Part of the Langenscheidt Publishing Group

CONTENTS

Introduction
About This Book   4
Recommended Tours For... 6

Overview
City Introduction   10
Food and Drink   14
Shopping   18
Entertainment   20
The Movies   22
History: Key Dates   24

Walks and Tours
1. Fisherman's Wharf   28
2. Alcatraz   33

3. North Beach and
   Telegraph Hill   36
4. Chinatown   41
5. South of Market
   and Union Square   47
6. Civic Center and
   Hayes Valley   53
7. Nob Hill and
   Russian Hill   58
8. Japantown, Pacific
   Heights, Cow Hollow 64
9. Golden Gate Park and
   Haight-Ashbury   70
10. The Castro   76
11. The Mission District   79

12. Fort Mason and
    the Marina   84
13. Golden Gate
    Promenade   87
14. Berkeley   90

Directory
A–Z   96
Accommodations   108
Restaurants   114
Entertainment   120

Credits and Index
Picture Credits   124
Index   126

Above: San Francisco highlights.

ABOUT THIS BOOK

This *Step by Step Guide* has been produced by the editors of Insight Guides, whose books have set the standard for visual travel guides since 1970. With top-quality photography and authoritative recommendations, this guidebook brings you the very best of San Francisco in a series of 14 tailor-made tours.

WALKS AND TOURS

The tours in the book provide something to suit all budgets, tastes, and trip lengths. As well as covering San Francisco's many classic attractions, the routes also take in lesser-known sights and up-and-coming areas; there is also an excursion to Berkeley for those who want to extend their visit outside San Francisco. The tours embrace a range of interests, so whether you are a nature-lover, an art or architecture fan, a shopaholic, or have kids to entertain, you will find an option to suit.

We recommend that you read the whole of a tour before setting out. This should help you to familiarize yourself with the route and enable you to plan where to stop for refreshments; options are shown in the 'Food and Drink' boxes, recognizable by the knife-and-fork symbol, on most pages.

For our pick of the walks by theme, consult Recommended Tours For... *(see pp.6–7).*

OVERVIEW

The tours are set in context by this introductory section, giving an overview of the city to set the scene, as well as background information on food and drink, shopping, and entertainment. A succinct history timeline in this chapter highlights the key events that have shaped San Francisco over the centuries.

DIRECTORY

Also supporting the tours is a Directory chapter, comprising a user-friendly, clearly organized A–Z of practical information, our pick of where to stay while you are in the city, and select restaurant listings; these eateries complement the usually more low-key cafés and restaurants that feature within the tours themselves and are intended to offer a wider choice for evening dining. Also included in this chapter are entertainment listings.

The Authors

Barbara Rockwell is a freelance arts and travel writer and devoted city-lover. Born and raised in the San Francisco Bay Area, she studied at the University of California at Berkeley before settling in San Francisco. Her U.S. travel expertise runs from coast to coast. She has written for various travel and lifestyle websites and contributed to Insight Guides' *Smart Guide San Francisco.*

Some of the tours in this book were originally conceived by Berkeley-based writer Anne Cherian.

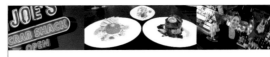

Margin Tips
Shopping tips, historical facts, handy hints, and information on activities help visitors to make the most of their time in San Francisco.

Feature Boxes
Notable topics are highlighted in these special boxes.

Key Facts Box
This box gives details of the distance covered on the tour, plus an estimate of how long it should take. It also states where the route starts and finishes, and gives key travel information such as which days are best to do the route or handy transport tips.

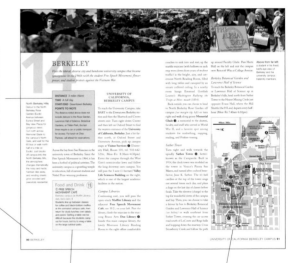

Footers
Look here for the tour name, a map reference and the main attraction on the double-page.

Food and Drink
Recommendations of where to stop for refreshments are given in these boxes. The numbers preceding each restaurant/café name link to references in the main text. On city maps, restaurants are plotted.

The $ signs at the end of each entry reflect the approximate cost of a three-course meal for one, with a half-bottle of house wine, not including tax and tip. These should be seen as a guide only. Price ranges, also quoted on the inside back flap for easy reference, are:

$$$$ above 100 U.S. dollars
$$$ 50–100 U.S. dollars
$$ 25–50 U.S. dollars
$ below 25 U.S. dollars

Route Map
Detailed cartography shows the itinerary clearly plotted with numbered dots. For more detailed mapping, see the pull-out map slotted inside the back cover.

ARCHITECTURE BUFFS

Survey stately mansions crowning Pacific Heights hills (walk 8), grand hotels and a Gothic cathedral atop Nob Hill (walk 7), the Beaux Arts buildings in Civic Center (walk 6), modern museums in South of Market (walk 5), and charming Victorians and Edwardians in the Haight and the Castro (walks 9 and 10).

RECOMMENDED TOURS FOR...

ART ENTHUSIASTS

Explore museum-rich South of Market for modern, folk, and cartoon art and varied cultural and historical museums (walk 5). Venture to Civic Center for the Asian Art Museum (walk 6), Golden Gate Park for the de Young (walk 9), or the Mission for colorful murals on Balmy Alley and the Women's Building (walk 11).

CAFÉ CULTURE

Chill with musicians at the Mission's Revolution Café (walk 11), sip espresso with modern-day bohemians at Caffe Trieste (walk 3), or people-watch in the Castro neighborhood from Café Flore (walk 10).

CHILDREN

Enjoy barking sea lions, an aquarium, and antique penny-arcade games at Fisherman's Wharf (walk 1); explore Zeum's multimedia museum (walk 5) and the Exploratorium's interactive exhibits for kids of all ages (walk 12); or rent rowboats and pedal boats at Stow Lake after visiting the vintage merry-go-round at one of the country's oldest playgrounds in Golden Gate Park (walk 9).

CHURCHES AND TEMPLES

See the old Mission Dolores that gave the Mission District its name (walk 11), tiny temples and California's first cathedral in Chinatown (walk 4), the Gothic Grace Cathedral on the crest of Nob Hill (walk 7), and Saints Peter and Paul Church, a popular site for Italian weddings in North Beach (walk 3).

FOODIES

Soak up North Beach's Italian heritage with pastas, focaccia, espresso, and *cannoli* pastries (walk 3), then shop the nearby Ferry Building's gourmet food purveyors and Saturday farmers' market. Visit the Mission for burritos (walk 11), Fisherman's Wharf for fresh seafood (walk 1), and the central neighborhoods for chic eateries (walks 7 and 8).

LITERARY TYPES

Pay homage to Beat writers in North Beach (walk 3), rifle through anarchist literature in the counterculture Haight (walk 9), explore a youth literary center on Mission Street that doubles as a pirate store (walk 11), and see the lovely inspiration for Armistead Maupin's Barbary Lane high on Russian Hill (walk 7).

PARKS AND GARDENS

Enjoy Golden Gate Park's lakes, trails, and botanical gardens (walk 9); hang with hipsters at the Mission's Dolores Park (walk 11); fly kites on the waterfront and relax by a swan-filled lagoon at the Palace of Fine Arts (walk 12); or picnic with a view at a Pacific Heights park (walk 8).

ROMANTICS

Explore garden-lined stairways before the city wakes (walks 3 and 7); retreat to a picnic-worthy nook in Golden Gate Park (walk 9); watch cable-cars roll by from a table for two on Hyde Street (walk 7); or take an evening amble along the northern waterfront to see the Golden Gate Bridge in the setting sun (walks 12 and 13).

SHOPPERS

Peruse Union Square's emporia and luxury outposts (walk 5), Jackson Square's antiques (walk 3), Hayes Street's unique boutiques (walk 6), high-end home decor and clothing on Fillmore and Union streets (walk 8), independent lines and one-of-a-kind curiosity shops in the Mission (walk 11), and music shops, funky fashions, and secondhand thrift in the Haight (walk 9).

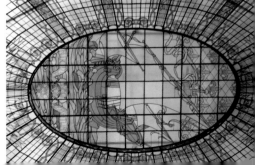

OVERVIEW

An overview of San Francisco's geography, customs, and culture, plus illuminating background information on food and drink, shopping, entertainment, and key historical dates.

INTRODUCTION   10

FOOD AND DRINK   14

SHOPPING   18

ENTERTAINMENT   20

THE MOVIES   22

HISTORY: KEY DATES   24

INTRODUCTION

Built on sloping hills and surrounded by sparkling waters, San Francisco is often called the most beautiful American city. Many visitors are also drawn west by the allure of the city's open-minded character, fertile ground for idealists and entrepreneurial gold-prospectors alike.

Big on Bridges
The Golden Gate Bridge is perhaps the most photographed bridge in the world. Crews continually work on maintenance, sandblasting rust and repainting from one end to the other. On the other side of the bay, the Bay Bridge connects the city to Oakland, and is the longest high-level steel bridge in the world, not to mention one of its busiest.

With dramatic scenic beauty, world-class cuisine, a plethora of cultural attractions, vibrant neighborhoods, and liberal locals, San Francisco is an easy city to love. Often thought of as the most European of American cities as well as the prettiest, San Francisco encompasses 43 windswept and fog-capped hills. These slopes afford arresting vistas of prominent bridges, sparkling blue waters, a varied skyline, and urban landscape. Landmarks such as cable-cars, Alcatraz, the Golden Gate Bridge, Mission Dolores, the sprawling Golden Gate Park, and the largest Chinatown in the U.S. all contribute to the unique, alluring charm of the City by the Bay.

CITY DEVELOPMENT

San Francisco is no stranger to the spotlight on the world's stage. Throughout the city's history, more than one boom and bust has drawn international attention. In the 19th century, the discovery of gold in the Sierra foothills ignited the largest mass migration in history, with treasure-seekers flooding the then small town of 2,000 and turning it into a proper city of 10 times that size. In 1906, the world's attention was

drawn to San Francisco when it was struck by a massive earthquake measuring an estimated 8.3 on the Richter scale. Coupled with the ensuing fire that raged for three days, the earthquake left the city in ruins. Then, later in the 20th century, the San Francisco Bay Area witnessed first-hand the prosperous dot-com era and its subsequent rapid unraveling.

Center Stage

The city has also attracted attention for its significant role in political moments and countercultural movements. The stage of the War Memorial Opera House saw the signing of the United Nations permanent charter in 1945. Then, in the late 1950s, North Beach became Beat-central, attracting writers such as Jack Kerouac, Allen Ginsberg, Lawrence Ferlinghetti, Philip Whalen, and Michael McClure.

In 1967, thousands of hippies descended on Haight-Ashbury and Golden Gate Park during the "Summer of Love." More recently, the city has become a focal point for the gay community's battles for equal rights; when Mayor Gavin Newsome began signing same-sex marriage licenses in 2004, the gay marriage issue became a national talking point.

Contemporary Appeal

Yet, no matter what dramas befall this city, its charms only seem to grow. Millions of visitors come each year to absorb San Francisco's legacy, explore Alcatraz, admire stunning views, dine on first-class cuisine, shop to their hearts' content, and climb impossibly steep hills in the city's iconic cable-cars. Whichever aspect of San Francisco intrigues, most visitors find it is difficult not to leave one's heart here.

GEOGRAPHY

At just 7 square miles (18sq km) and with a population of around 800,000, San Francisco is small for a major city in terms of both geography and population. Yet, for a city of such narrow limits, San Francisco covers a huge spectrum of natural and social terrain. The city sits on a bay over 400 square miles (1,000sq km) in area, which is crossed by five bridges. One of these bridges is the world-famous Golden Gate Bridge, which was completed in 1937 and still remains an enduring, defining symbol of San Francisco. Space in the compact city is at a premium today, with real-estate prices among the highest in the country.

Diverse Neighborhoods

There is a very strong sense of neighborhood in San Francisco, with locals taking immense pride in their home and promoting a stronger sense of community than is found in many other cities of similar stature. There are over a dozen neighborhood enclaves, each with a distinct culture and identity, including the bustling Chinatown, multicultural North Beach, gritty Tenderloin, Latino- and hipster-dominated Mission, well-maintained and gay-friendly Castro, laid-back and alternative Haight-Ashbury, upper-crust Pacific Heights,

Above from far left: Golden Gate Bridge; members of San Francisco's gay community; slanted parking; young San Franciscan in a fashionable bar.

"Painted Ladies" San Francisco is home to many fine Victorian houses, but the ones that feature most frequently on postcards are the "Painted Ladies", also dubbed "postcard row." These grand old buildings *(illustrated on p.8–9)* are located by Alamo Square, which is bordered by Fulton and Hayes streets at Scott. It's a pleasant hillside park (although best visited by day), with a view not only of these brightly colored homes and the skyscrapers downtown, but also within sight of the Civic Center.

Left: bird's-eye view of San Francisco.

tony Russian Hill, old-fashioned Nob Hill, and preppy, post-collegiate Marina and Cow Hollow. San Francisco's outlying districts are equally distinctive. For instance, the vast, residential Sunset and Richmond districts are home to many Russian, Irish, and Chinese families, and offer commercial hubs filled with bookstores, grocery stores, and Asian restaurants. The Richmond is also bisected by Lincoln Park, home to the Palace of the Legion of Honor, wild coastline trails, and arresting views of the Golden Gate Bridge.

CLIMATE

The city's climate is generally agreeable, but can vary from hour to hour and even between neighborhoods. Spring is warm and sunny, while summer is cooler and overcast, with the city often blanketed in fog. Come the fall, the city's real summer swings into effect, with beautifully mild and sunny days. The majority of the rainfall occurs in December and January, though crisp, sunny days offer respite from those that are damp and overcast.

Contrary to the common misconception of a lush California, much of the state is, in fact, a semi-desert. Its Mediterranean climate, where 98 percent of its annual rainfall occurs between November and March, leaves it vulnerable to drought and wildfires the rest of the year. Still, these natural hazards, along with the possibility of earthquakes and the reality of frequent fog, only seem to add to the city's magnetic charm.

Above: San Franciscan portraits.

Earthquakes

From its plunging cliffs to its dramatic peaks and valley, the astounding natural beauty of the Bay Area is the result of shifting tectonic plates. Sitting between two major seismic fault lines – the San Andreas skirting the edge of the city and the Hayward running up the East Bay – San Francisco is continually under threat of jolts that can cause millions of dollars' worth of damage. Fortunately, improved building codes and "retrofitting" (structural revamping) have stabilized many bridges, highway overpasses, and downtown buildings that suffered in previous quakes.

Despite the threat, San Franciscans handle the subject of earthquakes with great aplomb, shrugging their shoulders with a "What can you do about it?" attitude. Still, every California school kid learns the basic rules: if an earthquake occurs, stay indoors, preferably under something sturdy like a piece of furniture or in a doorframe; if outside, avoid trees, power lines, buildings, and bridges.

THE PEOPLE

San Francisco is truly a multicultural city, with diverse demographics representing all ethnicities and proclivities. The Chinatown area is famous, but San Francisco also has a vibrant Hispanic-origin population and large communities of people of Italian, Japanese, Russian, and Southeast Asian descent. Indeed, only 35 percent of San Franciscans were born in California, while 39 percent were

born outside of the U.S. San Francisco is known internationally for its large gay and lesbian population, which crosses all ethnic divisions and wields significant political power in the city. Many are attracted to San Francisco by its liberal, accommodating spirit. Tolerance is part of the city's ethos, not to mention public policy: tolerance of cultural, religious, racial, and gender divergences are hard-wired into the city's civic codes and legislation.

Living Standards

The general standard of living is high, and the average earnings of residents enable enough eating out and nights on the town to sustain the city's eating and cultural establishments. However, it is estimated that San Francisco has the highest number of homeless people per capita in the country. Recent initiatives are making a difference, but visitors will undoubtedly notice the many down-and-outs.

HEALTH AND ENVIRONMENT

San Francisco has rightly developed a reputation for being very eco-friendly, with a broad recycling program, a significant bike-riding population, some of the world's toughest anti-pollution laws, and countless campaigns to "green" the city by planting trees and native species on rooftops and in public places. Nevertheless, it is also a densely populated metropolitan area that carries inevitable environmental concerns, ranging from air quality to water shortages.

San Franciscans are also notoriously concerned with the health of their bodies and souls. There is an abundance of yoga studios, natural food stores, alternative health practitioners, and vegetarian restaurants, and the city is home to the first Buddhist training monastery outside of Asia.

Recreation

Having a good time is an easy order to obey in the city that lays claim to the first espresso on the West Coast and to being the home of the Martini. The rich nightlife, food, and cultural pickings ensure that foodies, politicos, film buffs, aspiring poets, jazz fiends, barhoppers, and 1960s nostalgists all have plenty to enjoy.

The city is home to diverse museums, with the majority clustered downtown and in the South of Market district, although a number are strewn about outlying neighborhoods. The heavy-hitters include the San Francisco Museum of Modern Art (SFMOMA), the Legion of Honor, the de Young, and the Asian Art Museum. In addition, there are many museums celebrating San Francisco's history and its ethnically diverse population.

Fresh-air enthusiasts are also spoiled for choice in San Francisco, with nearly every kind of outdoor activity on offer, from sailing and windsurfing on the bay to biking, baseball, basketball, tennis, polo, and fly-fishing in the sprawling Golden Gate Park, the urban oasis that stretches 52 city blocks from the Haight-Ashbury neighborhood to the ocean.

Above from far left: Chinatown paper lanterns; the Beat Museum documents the city in the mid-20th century; bridge in the Japanese Tea Garden, Golden Gate Park; walking the dog near Golden Gate Promenade.

Gay Capital
Fort Mason was an important point of embarcation and disembarcation during World War II; many of the American soldiers and sailors who passed through chose to stay on in the city following a "dishonorable discharge" and indeed at the end of the war. The community they began evolved and made San Francisco into what many people consider to be the gay capital of the U.S.

FOOD AND DRINK

California cuisine, cultural diversity, celebrity chefs, and bounty from the sea and land – the City by the Bay is a gourmet's delight, with a varied and voracious appetite that should appeal to foodies of all culinary persuasions.

California Cuisine
"California cuisine" is typified by seasonal, usually organic, local produce. Flavor combinations accentuate freshness, subtlety, and texture, and meat is not always the focal point.

Nothing has changed since the writer Alice B. Toklas referred in 1954 to her San Francisco dining experiences with her partner Gertrude Stein as "gastronomic orgies." The city continues to delight food-and-drink-lovers, and has emerged as one of the culinary capitals of the world. Blessed with year-round natural abundance, thriving immigrant communities, and a slight spirit of rebellion, San Francisco appeals to all tastes. Authentic ethnic eateries serve dishes from cultures all over the globe, and the hugely popular California cuisine promotes the use of locally grown, in-season ingredients. From fresh breads and delicate pastries at cafés to delectable small plates at esteemed fine-dining establishments courtesy of celebrity chefs, the extensive menu of enticements is virtually impossible to abstain from in this "Paris of the West."

INTERNATIONAL FLAVORS

San Francisco's international gastronomic influences began early on. From the mid-19th century, immigrants contributed considerable diversity to the city's culinary character: adding to the Mexican and American traditions already present, Chinese, French, Irish, German, Basque, Spanish, and Italian immigrants brought with them the tastes of home – dishes such as *Cioppino*, a fish stew that Italian fishermen brought with them from Genoa and adapted by using the sea's bounty from San Francisco Bay.

Right: one of many Japanese restaurants in the city.

To this day, immigrants continue to introduce dishes that broaden the city's palate, as evidenced by the city's Ethiopian, Arabian, Moroccan, Afghan, and Turkish restaurants. Thanks to San Francisco's position on the edge of the Pacific Ocean, its pan-Asian and Pacific Rim cuisine remains especially strong and diverse.

SUSTAINABLE FOOD MOVEMENT

The Bay Area is very well known for its attention to health and the environment. It is unsurprising, then, that celebrity chefs and food artisans have in recent years managed to turn the region into the epicenter of the American sustainable food movement. This is based on the belief that food should be produced locally and using techniques based on age-old traditions. Chef Alice Waters is credited with starting this culinary revolution; in 1971 she gave birth to "California cuisine," *(see margin tip, left)* when she opened the now-famous Chez Panisse restaurant in Berkeley. The cuisine highlights the Bay Area's natural cornucopia, and its wild popularity has resulted in an impressive assortment of boutique charcuteries, cheese makers, bakeries, and superb farmers' markets.

PLACES TO EAT

Cafés
San Francisco loves its café culture: the importance to locals of Italian-style, espresso-based coffee, mouth-watering light meals, and ready Wi-Fi access should not be underestimated. In addition to excellent coffee and teas, most cafés also offer a menu of sandwiches, salads, soups, bagels, breakfast muffins, and pastries. Specialty teas are also popular, and are found in cafés as well as teahouses. Downtown, especially in the Financial District, major coffee chains are ubiquitous, but in other neighborhoods local independent coffee roasters and cafés thrive. Even at 11am on a Wednesday, cafés are crowded with local laptop-toting freelance workers; their fondness for camping out for hours at a time can sometimes make finding space a challenge.

Neighborhood Bars and Eateries
Neighborhood restaurants run the gamut from hole-in-the-wall Thai or sushi spots to trendy white-tablecloth affairs, and from friendly French bistros

Chocolate Heaven

Whether you crave Belgian buttercreams or Swiss champagne truffles, San Francisco can come to your rescue. Choose from more than 150 kinds of premium chocolate bars from around the world at Fog City News (www.fogcitynews.com), feast on a giant sundae in Ghirardelli Square *(see p.32)*, or sip a deliciously rich hot chocolate drink at Bittersweet *(see p.65)*. Local artisan chocolate boutiques are also perfect for finding one-of-a-kind indulgences or lavish gifts. Recchiutti (www.recchiutti.com) offers exquisite confections featuring drawings from local artists, XOX Truffles (www.xoxtruffles.com) sells sweet, tiny, handmade, flavored truffles, and Joseph Schmidt Confections (www.joseph schmidtconfections.com) dispenses mouth-watering signature egg-shaped truffles.

Dress Codes

Despite the city's obsession with food, dining in San Francisco is rarely a fancy affair, and few restaurants have dress codes. Only the ritzy, top-notch restaurants truly merit dress-up attire, though in some mid-range restaurants you may feel more comfortable in something a step up from T-shirt and sneakers.

to even friendlier German beer halls. Small-plate restaurants are particularly growing in popularity. Many bars also have a kitchen serving either pub fare or more upscale snacks and small plates, depending on the establishment.

High-End Restaurants

From French to fusion, the menus at San Francisco's hottest tables are first-class, and you will need to reserve, often far in advance. The highest concentration of fine dining is found downtown, from the Financial District to the Embarcadero and South of Market. However, many top-notch restaurants are on the backstreets or scattered in far-flung neighborhoods. For excellent, bang up-to-the-minute advice, the concierge of a fancy hotel is always a good bet, or check out www.yelp.com, http://sfeater.com, as well as www.opentable.com.

WHAT TO EAT

Around the city, many neighborhoods are known for a particular cuisine. The Mission's many *taquerías* offer raved-about burritos, North Beach serves Italian and excellent espresso, Polk Street has a high concentration of small Thai restaurants, the Tenderloin is known for Indian and Vietnamese food, and while Chinatown is an easy choice for Chinese, the Richmond District's Clement Street is also filled with authentic fare that is sometimes harder to find among Chinatown's tourist traps. Fisherman's Wharf is always crowded with seafood-lovers, but mid-November through May is particularly busy, with locals enticed by Dungeness crabs steamed, cracked, drowned in butter, and accompanied by San Francisco's famous sourdough bread. Throughout the city, plenty of attention is paid to vegetarians and even vegans, even in restaurants that also serve meat.

EATING PATTERNS

On weekdays, breakfast is generally between 7am and 10am. In all corners of the city, people line up for morning

lattes to bring to work. On weekends, lines wrap around corners all morning for leisurely brunches, with service running into the early afternoon. Brunch can be a hearty affair, from omelets with fresh veggies and cheeses to pancakes with fruit. Those with a lighter appetite nibble on pastries and bagels at cafés, and are not shy about lingering hours to read the newspaper and catch up with friends. Weekday lunch is between 11:30am and 2:30pm and dinner starts around 5:30pm, although locals rarely venture out to dinner before 7pm and few restaurants seat past 10pm.

DRINKING CULTURE

San Franciscans love their libations. Surrounded by wine country, the city is a convenient gateway for visiting the many acclaimed vineyards in its vicinity and trying an excellent selection of local wine, from traditional varietals such as Chardonnay and Cabernet, to lesser-known specialties such as Gamay Beaujolais. The proximity to wine country also means San Francisco is filled with well-informed wine critics, and those aspiring to be so. Wine bars are increasingly popular, especially in the central neighborhoods and downtown.

If beer is your beverage, there are many drinking establishments in San Francisco where it is the clear focus. As well as Belgian beer bars and Guinness-pouring Irish pubs, the city has several large, industrial brewpubs. Residents began brewing their own beer early on in the city's history, and

nowadays there are microbreweries producing beers with the strength and complexity to rival any cocktail or glass of wine. One of the standouts is the Anchor Steam Brewery, which not only makes beer, but gin and rye bourbon as well.

Cocktails are no humdrum affair either, with "mixologists" behind the bars at destinations such as the Alembic, Bourbon and Branch, and Rye turning out Sazeracs, Pisco Sours, cucumber and basil gimlets, and other exceptionally creative and tasty concoctions.

Above from far left: bright lights of the bar; top-notch presentation; the city is famed for its great coffee; irresistible chocolate dessert.

Opposite below: smart vegetarian dish.

Daily Bread

Bread has long been a San Francisco specialty. With yeast in short supply, settlers who arrived in the Gold Rush utilized fermented dough as the basis of their bread. This technique hardly originated with this generation of gold-seekers, but San Francisco is home to natural yeasts and air-borne bacteria that create the chewy texture and sour taste that define San Franciscan sourdough. In addition to sourdough from Boudin at the Wharf *(see p.28)*, locals get their daily bread from many local bakeries. North Beach's Liguria Bakery *(see p.39)* is a favorite for focaccia, and Stella Pastry and Café Bakery (446 Columbus Avenue at Green) is beloved for its *sacripantina*. Boulangerie Bay bread *(see p.115)* has six outposts serving fresh organic breads and French pastries, and Tartine Bakery *(see p.81)* is a Mission must for tasty tarts.

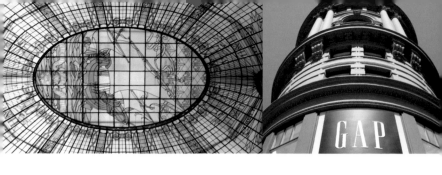

SHOPPING

Something for everyone is found downtown among the modern shopping centers, affordable retail outposts, and international luxury designers, while boutique-lined streets in other neighborhoods cater to distinctive kinds of shopping wish lists.

Opening Times
Stores are generally open Monday to Saturday from around 11am–6pm, and Sunday from around noon–6pm. However, calling in advance to check store hours is wise, especially with smaller boutiques.

When the shopping urge strikes, San Francisco is an excellent city to be in. Far-flung tastes are satisfied by a cosmopolitan spread of merchandise that includes gourmet foods, antiques and artwork, whimsical home decor, designer fashions, secondhand thrift, music, literature, and offbeat gifts galore.

LOCAL DESIGN

As the birthplace of blue jeans and behemoth Gap Inc., it is no surprise that San Francisco's fashion sense is dominated by denim and other casuals. Still, the common ultra-relaxed look is joined by others that up the fashion ante a bit. Hipster haunts in the Mission and Haight neighborhoods are swarmed by frightfully cool twenty- and thirtysomethings in edgy, attitude-laced outfits, while the smart central neighborhoods are strolled by carefully coifed urban sophisticates in preppy and Euro-chic designer outfits.

San Francisco has a strong independent design culture, evidenced not only by the locally made clothing, jewelry, accessories, housewares, and crafts carried by boutiques, but also by the large turnout at design and shopping fairs that are held throughout the year such as Capsule

SF (www.capsulesf.com), where local designers showcase and sell cutting-edge work to fashion-savvy city dwellers. Excellent local independent designers include Dema, House of Hengst, Minnie Wilde, and Sunhee Moon, all of which have stores in the Mission *(see pp.79–83)*. San Francisco Fashion Week (www.fashionweek-sf.com), launched in 2004, continues to gain steam.

WHERE TO SHOP

Downtown
San Francisco's shopping pulse thumps most wildly in the Union Square neighborhood. Streets are stacked with elegant emporia (Saks Fifth Avenue, Neiman Marcus, Barney's New York, and Nordstrom and Bloomingdales inside the Westfield Centre) and glossy boutiques for international designers such as Betsey Johnson, Cartier, Chanel, Coach, Gucci, Hermès, Louis Vuitton, Prada, Thomas Pink, and Wilkes Bashford. Also here are major American retail outposts and San Francisco institutions such as Gumps, Scheuer Linens, and Britex Fabrics.

For the best selection of antiques, head to historic Jackson Square (tel: 398-8155; www.jacksonsquaresf.com).

Another Financial District shopping destination is the four-towered Embarcadero Center (Sacramento Street between Battery and Drumm streets), a blend of flower-potted patios, wide walkways, eateries, and familiar retail faces. Nearby, the Ferry Building is a go-to for gourmets and high-end homebodies, with upscale food purveyors, home and garden shops, and an outstanding farmers' market on Saturdays and Wednesdays.

Central Neighborhoods

Pacific Heights' Fillmore Street (between Post and Pacific) and Presidio Heights' Sacramento Street (between Lyon and Maple) offer a wealth of luxury delicacies, particularly high-end clothing and interior-decor shops. If European shoes, Florentine soaps, and vintage French furnishings are out of your budget, these are still picturesque streets in which to window-shop.

Also devoid of chains, Hayes Street (between Franklin and Laguna) in Hayes Valley is a cheerfully artsy and unique mix of art galleries, cafés, eateries, and boutiques supplying posh European footwear, tasty travel accessories, handsome home furnishings, and upscale men's body products.

Sophisticated clusters of jewelry shops, mainstream beauty outlets, clothing boutiques, and chic eateries make Cow Hollow one of the most popular high-end shopping destinations in the city. Try Union Street (between Franklin and Steiner) and Chestnut (from Fillmore Street to Divisadero). Down in Japantown, the Japan Center *(see p.64)* supplies everything from vintage silk kimonos to culinary ingredients.

Other Neighborhoods

Upper Haight offers a scruffy jumble of secondhand, vintage, and contemporary clothing stores, plus trendy shoe shops, independent music stores, and head shops selling all manner of smoking paraphernalia.

In the Castro, expect to find fashionable men's clothing and gay-oriented specialty stores, and the nation's largest gay-and-lesbian-themed bookstore.

The Misson, meanwhile, offers varied offbeat fare: ethnic threads, Latin jazz CDs, refurbished furniture, fedoras and porkpies, politico literature, unusual housewares, independent designer boutiques, and curiosity shops.

North of Market Street, Chinatown is a bustling bazaar year-round, brimming with tea-selling apothecaries, sidewalk souvenir racks, cramped shops, and fresh-produce stands. Tourists flood Grant Avenue while locals grocery-shop on Stockton Street.

Further north, artsy bookstores, chocolate truffles, Italian bakeries and delicatessens, European lingerie, premium denim, flirty dresses, quaint curios, and antique maps are the order of the day in North Beach.

The other side of Columbus Avenue in posh Russian Hill, Polk Street offers high-end progressive women's fashion, lacy lingerie, vintage and consignment fare; as it heads south for the Tenderloin, low-end clothing and other eclectic stores are more common.

Above from far left: the Neiman Marcus store in Union Square; Gap hails from San Francisco; local art gallery; Levi's, another homegrown giant.

ENTERTAINMENT

San Francisco is home to world-class dance, theater, opera, symphony companies, and dozens of clubs. And because of its diminutive size, most forms of entertainment are only a walk or a bus ride away from the city center.

Free Festivals
San Francisco's tradition of congregating in parks for entertainment continues to this day. Free Shakespeare in the Park spotlights works by the Bard each summer, and aria-admirers turn out in droves to Golden Gate Park each fall for a relaxed, cultured afternoon of Free Opera in the Park.

San Franciscans are an adventurous and diverse lot where entertainment is concerned. The city is rich with artistic types and well-informed critics who nurture a vibrant cultural scene that includes both traditional artistic expressions such as opera, symphony, and ballet, and also more avant-garde forms. With its open-minded atmosphere and taste for pushing boundaries, the Bay Area has particularly built a reputation for itself as a breeding ground for experimental and often outrageous work.

MUSIC

Classical and Opera
San Francisco has long cherished classical music. In the city's early days, this passion was so great that fire brigades escorted favorite divas through the crowds to performances. San Francisco soon became a regular stop for European troupes, and the tradition still continues: today there are no fewer than seven opera companies in the Bay Area. There are also more classical concerts per capita here than in any other city in the country, a phenomenon described by one critic as an "unreasonable profusion." Chamber music is well served too, with peaceful churches often hosting the small, talented groups.

Jazz
The Lower Fillmore neighborhood was undoubtedly once the city's hopping hotbed of jazz music. During the 1940s it became known as the "Harlem of the West," attracting legends such as Ella Fitzgerald, Duke Ellington, Billie Holiday, Charles Mingus, and Charlie Parker. Today the Fillmore is home to the San Francisco outpost of Yoshi's – a very well-respected Oakland jazz club – but jazz clubs are also found in other parts of the city, including downtown and North Beach.

Contemporary
The city is no stranger to staying on top of current music trends. Light shows held at the Fillmore and Avalon Ballroom became the standard for rock gigs all around the world. In the 1960s locally based artists including Grateful Dead, Jefferson Airplane, and Janis Joplin regularly appeared at these venues, and performed in high-profile concerts in Golden Gate Park. Now, the Bay Area's eclectic music scene includes everything from electronica to indie pop, home-grown hyphy, and hip-hop. Large venues include the Warfield Theater, the Fillmore, Great American Music Hall, and Slims; more intimate venues are also popular.

THEATER

San Francisco's early theater tradition started with a proliferation of melodeons (theater-bar-music halls) but more "serious" theater picked up at the turn of the 20th century. In 1967, director Bill Ball led the American Conservatory Theater to its San Francisco premiere, and it soon become a theater with a national reputation. Today, the theater district is centered just west of Union Square on Geary Street, and offers a brilliant spectrum of theatrical flavors. Major commercial theaters stage Broadway hits, while non-profits such as the Magic Theater push new pieces and playwrights, and also premieres early works by major playwrights such as Sam Shepard.

Come fall, the San Francisco Fringe Festival serves up untraditional and uncensored fare.

BARS AND CLUBS

San Francisco nightlife options are across the board, from Union Square hotel bars to Irish pubs, punk-rock dives, cozy wine bars, intimate comedy venues, and large dance clubs. Live bands and local DJs spin for varied tastes at smaller venues, while more massive clubs draw international DJs. Many of these nightspots are hybrid affairs, blurring the lines between bars, lounges, and clubs. The liveliest neighborhoods after nightfall are the Mission District, the Marina, South of Market, and North Beach.

Festivals

January: Dine About Town; Noir City Film Festival

February: Noise Pop; Lunar New Year Parade; Independent Film Festival; Spike and Mike's Festival of Animation

March: Anarchist Book Fair; St Patrick's Day Parade

April: Perpetual Indulgence in the Park; Cherry Blossom Festival

May: Cinco de Mayo; San Francisco International Film Festival; Bay to Breakers; Carnaval; Mission Creek Music and Arts Festival

June: San Francisco International LGBT Film Festival; North Beach Street Fair; Haight Street Fair; Pride Parade, Free Shakespeare in the Park

July: Silent Film Festival; AIDS Walk

August: San Francisco Jewish Film Festival; Stern Grove Festival

September: Fringe Festival; Free Opera in the Park; Folsom Street Fair; SF Shakespeare Festival; Ghirardelli Square Chocolate Festival

October: Litquake; Castro Street Fair; Hardly Strictly Bluegrass Festival

November: Dia de los Muertos

December: Dance Along Nutcracker

THE MOVIES

San Francisco's iconic views have played supporting roles in movies of all genres. Francis Ford Coppola has his headquarters here, and George Lucas has taken up residence in the Presidio.

Coppola and Lucas

"Just say Francis Coppola is up in San Francisco in an old warehouse making films," announced Coppola in 1971. Two years before, he and fellow upstart George Lucas left Hollywood to start their own studio, American Zoetrope. Lucas now has 1,300 employees at his Skywalker Ranch in nearby Nicasio and other Marin County locations. His $2-billion business includes the *Star Wars* movies, *Indiana Jones*, the THX sound system, and Industrial Light & Magic. Lucas's San Francisco home is the Letterman Arts campus, in the coveted Presidio near the Golden Gate Bridge.

Early moving images were captured in northern California in the late 19th century by Eadweard Muybridge and Thomas Edison, and San Francisco has been a magnet for movie-makers ever since. With its range of romantically iconic views and backdrops. the city has long offered high-value locations for directors. Barbra Streisand deftly maneuvered her Volkswagen between two cable-cars in *What's Up Doc?* (1972); Kim Novak hurled herself from a (non-existent) tower in *Vertigo* (1958) against a backdrop of the Golden Gate Bridge; and Steve McQueen bounced a Mustang over the city's hills in *Bullitt* (1968). More recently, bad mutants inventively used the Golden Gate Bridge against good mutants to win the spectacular battle over a genetic facility located (digitally) on Alcatraz in *X-Men: The Last Stand* (2006).

A MOVIE-MAKING TRADITION

San Francisco's movie associations date back to the 1920s with the silent movies *The Fog* (1923) and *Greed* (1924). Then came the talkies of the 1930s: Howard Hawks's *Barbary Coast* set in 1850s San Francisco and W.S. Van Dyke's *San Francisco*, which depicted the city col-lapsing in the 1906 earthquake. In 1941, John Huston's *The Maltese Falcon* had Humphrey Bogart, Peter Lorre, and Sydney Greenstreet skulking in the alleys and backways of Nob Hill. The Fairmont Hotel, atop the same hill, has featured in movies from *Vertigo* in 1958 to *Petulia* (with Julie Christie and George C. Scott) exactly a decade later, to the Sean Connery drama *The Rock* in 1996.

STAR LOCATIONS

Alcatraz *(see p.33)*, of course, has made regular appearances (*The Birdman of Alcatraz*, 1962; *Escape from Alcatraz*, 1979; *The Rock*, 1996), as has City Hall (*The Right Stuff*, 1983; *Class Action*, 1990) and the Golden Gate Bridge (*Superman*, 1978; *A View to a Kill*, 1985; *Interview with the Vampire*, 1994; and many more). The bridge, and Mission Dolores, provided backdrops for *Vertigo*, whose Madeleine Elster (Kim Novak) lives in the Empire Hotel (now the York Hotel) at 940 Sutter Street.

North Beach

The North Beach area is regularly jammed with lights, camera cranes, and trailers. The renowned Saints Peter and Paul Church on Washington

Square was the site of a shoot-out in 1971's *Dirty Harry*, and four blocks northwest, City Lights Bookstore was the setting for *Flashback*, a 1960s film starring a radical played by Dennis Hopper. The bookstore also featured in the 1980 Beat-inspired movie *Heart Beat* with Nick Nolte, Sissy Spacek, and John Hurt.

The Tosca Café, across the street at 242 Columbus Avenue, featured in *Basic Instinct*, starring Michael Douglas and Sharon Stone, as did the country-and-western bar Rawhide on 7th Street in South of Market.

Downtown
The Bank of America at 555 California Street became "America's tallest skyscraper" in 1974 as 86 fictional stories were added and then torched in Irwin Allen's disaster movie *The Towering Inferno*.

The Transamerica Pyramid *(see small picture on p.2, bottom left)*, one of the city's emblematic buildings, has featured in dozens of films, including the 1978 remake of the science-fiction movie *Invasion of the Body Snatchers*, shot by the hometown director Philip Kaufman. With the aid of time-lapse photography, director David Fincher used the pyramid, as well as a number of other buildings that transformed the city's skyline in the 1970s, to dramatic effect by chronicling its rise to convey the passage of time in his 2007 film, *Zodiac*.

Above from far left: famous chase through the streets of San Francisco in *Bullitt*; Humphrey Bogart in *The Maltese Falcon*.

Gay Outrage
Extra guards were needed on the sets of *Basic Instinct* (1992) to manage the daily protests by gay activists. They thought the script was homophobic and should be banned or censored.

Below: vertiginous Jimmy Stewart and Kim Novak.

HISTORY: KEY DATES

San Francisco's early history witnessed European colonialism, the discovery of gold, and an earthquake that changed the face of the city forever. The 1900s saw the influx of beatniks, hippies, yuppies, and, then the dot-com revolution.

SETTLEMENT AND FOUNDING

Early HIstory
In 8,000 B.C., the archaeological record shows that ancestors of the Ohlone and Miwok tribes were living on the sandy plains of what would later become San Francisco Bay.

1579	Sir Francis Drake lands north of the present-day Golden Gate Bridge.
1776	The Spanish arrive and the Misión San Francisco de Asís – now better known as Mission Dolores – is built.
1822	Mexico wins its independence from Spain; California becomes a Mexican territory.
1846	John Montgomery of the U.S.S. *Portsmouth* first raises the Stars and Stripes in present-day Portsmouth Square.
1847	The settlement of Yerba Buena is renamed San Francisco.

LATE 19TH CENTURY

1848	Gold is discovered in the Sierra Nevada foothills. The Treaty of Guadalupe Hildago is signed, making California American.
1849	Gold Rush sparks the greatest mass migration in history.
1850	U.S. Congress grants California statehood, skipping intermediate territory stage.
1869	Transcontinental Railroad is completed, making millionaires of "Big Four" barons Crocker, Huntington, Hopkins, and Stanford.
1870	William Hammond Hall begins turning the city's western sand dunes into Golden Gate Park.
1873	Cable Cars are invented.
1875	Anti-Chinese riots raze Chinatown.

20TH CENTURY

1906	On April 18, an earthquake (estimated to be an 8.3-magnitude) destroys much of the city and leaves thousands dead or homeless.
1910	Angel Island Immigration Station opens. Known as "the Ellis Island of the west," it will process 175,000 immigrants.
1915	Panama-Pacific Exposition is hosted in the area later christened the Marina.
1933	Coit Tower is completed.

1937	The Golden Gate Bridge opens, some six months after the Bay Bridge is completed.
1940	The Lower Fillmore jazz clubs attract greats such as Ella Fitzgerald, Duke Ellington, Billie Holiday, Charles Mingus, and Charlie Parker to the "Harlem of the west."
1941–5	Some 1.6 million American military personnel pass through Fort Mason, and the Bay Area's industry booms.
1945	The United Nations charter is signed in the War Memorial Opera House.
1955	Allen Ginsberg reads his poem *Howl* at Gallery Six, igniting the San Francisco Poetry Renaissance.
1957	San Francisco columnist Herb Caen coins the word "Beatnik."
1964	Nob Hill's Grace Cathedral is completed.
1965	The Grateful Dead debut at the Fillmore Auditorium.
1967	Haight-Ashbury blossoms in the "Summer of Love," making the city the center of the counterculture.
1971	Inspired by the Chicano civil rights movement, artists begin mural series on the Mission's Balmy Alley.
1972	Transamerica Pyramid completed.
1977	Harvey Milk is elected city supervisor, becoming the first openly gay person elected to public office in the U.S.
1978	Supervisor Harvey Milk and Mayor George Moscone are killed by former Supervisor Dan White.
1989	During the opening of the World Series at Candlestick Park, the 7.1-magnitude Loma Prieta earthquake rocks the Bay Area, killing 67 people and causing billions of dollars of damage.
1995	The "New Economy" of the dot-com era dominates much of San Francisco life *(see margin tip, right)*.

21ST CENTURY

2000	The San Francisco Giants open the new Pacific Bell Park stadium.
2003	200,000 San Franciscans are part of the largest international anti-war demonstration in history.
2004	Mayor Gavin Newsom issues marriage licenses for same-sex couples, putting this controversial issue on the national stage.
2005	The new de Young Museum opens in Golden Gate Park.
2006	San Francisco Representative Nancy Pelosi becomes the first woman elected Speaker of the House of Representatives.
2009	Work starts on the Transbay Terminal, the new hub of Northern Californian Transportation, due to be completed in 2014.

Dot-Com Boom and Bust

At the start of the 21st century, the future looked bright in San Francisco: nearby Silicon Valley invigorated established industries and spurred thousands of "start-up" companies, and venture capitalists threw money at shiny ideas, stock prices soared, and the housing market hit new heights. Recent college graduates had more money than they could count, but much of the prosperity owed more to innovative bookkeeping than business acumen: investors would never make it out of the red. The bubble burst on October 9, 2002, and many of the new "millionaires" returned home to their parents.

WALKS AND TOURS

1. Fisherman's Wharf   28

2. Alcatraz   33

3. North Beach and Telegraph Hill   36

4. Chinatown   41

5. South of Market

    and Union Square   47

6. Civic Center and Hayes Valley   53

7. Nob Hill and Russian Hill   58

8. Japantown, Pacific Heights,

    and Cow Hollow   64

9. Golden Gate Park

    and Haight-Ashbury   70

10. The Castro   76

11. The Mission District   79

12. Fort Mason and the Marina   84

13. Golden Gate Promenade   87

14. Berkeley   90

FISHERMAN'S WHARF

*Weave through the lively daytime crowds along seaside Fisherman's Wharf for
sunbathing sea lions, historic ships, a double-decker carousel, hot-fudge sundaes
and tchotchkes galore, then ride a creaky cable-car back downtown.*

Above: Fisherman's
Wharf sign; Boudin at
the Wharf.

Winter Residents

Endearingly known as
"Sea Lebrities," the
famous Pier 39 sea
lions first arrived in
January 1990 as a
herd of 10–15, but
within a few short
months, thanks to the
sheltered location and
plentiful herring supply,
the small gathering
had grown to a party
of 300. Now up to
900 sea lions stop in
for the winter.

DISTANCE 2 miles (3km)

TIME A half-day

START Pier 39

END Ghirardelli Square

POINTS TO NOTE

The piers near Fisherman's Wharf are
also the place to catch a ferry to
Alcatraz and across the bay. This
tour begins at Pier 39 (Powell–Hyde
cable-car; Metro: F; bus: 15, 37, 49)

Food and Drink 🍴

① ALIOTO'S

8 Fisherman's Wharf; tel: 673-0183;
www.aliotos.com; daily L and D; $$
In San Francisco, the Alioto name
stands for politics, feuds, family,
and fine food. For generations, this
famous family-owned establishment
has ruled the Wharf with fresh, local
seafood and Sicilian dishes.

② BOUDIN AT THE WHARF

160 Jefferson Street; tel: 928-1849;
www.boudinbakery.com; daily B, L,
and D; $
The flagship location is the perfect
spot to try the tangy-flavored sour-
dough bread that the company
began baking back in 1849. Nosh
on classic sandwiches and soups in
indoor and outdoor seating. Upstairs
is the fancier Bistro Boudin (tel: 351-
5561; daily L and D; $$$) for upscale
pastas, seafood, and entrées.

Fisherman's Wharf is filled with
knick-knack stores, lively carnivalesque
attractions, and scores of tourists,
making it easy to forget that it represents the maritime past that is so
integral to San Francisco's character. In
the maritime present, it is still the
place to pick up a ferry to Alcatraz *(see
pp.33–5)* or Angel Island, as well as
across the bay.

Once you are back on dry land, if
crowds and trinkets hold no appeal,
visit the waterfront in the evening
when the stores have closed and everyone has gone home. Then, accompanied only by barking sea lions and the
city's lights on the bay, it is much easier
to enjoy the saltiness of this once-
bustling harbor.

PIER 39

Built from old wharves and anchoring
the 45-acre (18-hectare) wharf area,
Pier 39 ❶ is a major tourist attraction,
second only to Disneyland in California.
Young children can ride the colorful,
hand-painted vintage **San Francisco
Carousel**, where traditional leaping
horses and rocking chariots circle
beneath painted depictions of famous
local landmarks. Weave through the
decked plazas filled with kitsch and
head to the western side to see and hear

the playful squabbles of some of the city's most famed inhabitants: hundreds of boisterous **sea lions ❷**, which hang out on pontoons in the water below. Then, to get even closer to the bay's sea life, enter the nearby **Aquarium of the Bay ❸** (Pier 39; tel: 623-5300; www. aquariumofthebay.com; June–Aug: daily 9am–8pm, Sept–May: Mon–Fri 10am–6pm, Sat–Sun 10am–7pm; charge), home to some 20,000 local marine animals. Walk through the underwater glass tunnel to see sharks, fish, and crustaceans from a diver's-eye view.

SEAFOOD AND SOURDOUGH

Walk west on Jefferson Street, the principal drag of Fisherman's Wharf traversed by the F-Line's vintage streetcars on their way downtown and home to seafood street vendors hawking boiled shellfish and clam chowder in an edible sourdough bowl. Alternatively, for seafood, break at **Alioto's**, see ⑪①, or for some of that

classic San Francisco bread, stop at the flagship **Boudin at the Wharf ❹**, see ⑪②. Peer through sidewalk windows to see expert bakers working on loaves, baguettes, and more unusual shapes such as lobsters, alligators, and teddy bears. Upstairs, take a self-guided tour of the museum (daily noon–7pm; charge) and observe the bakery in full swing below.

JEFFERSON STREET ATTRACTIONS

This block of Jefferson Street is home two oddball attractions. Across the street from Boudin at No. 145 is the **Wax Museum ❺** (tel: 800-439-4305; www.waxmuseum.com; Mon–Fri 10am–9pm; charge), with its rather creepy cast of characters of some 250 wax figures, including a chamber of horrors, celebrities, and political figures. Just a few doors down is **Ripley's Believe It or Not! ❻** (175 Jefferson Street; tel: 771-6188; www.ripleysf.

Above from far left:
Pier 39 flag; several of the city's famous noisy sea lions.

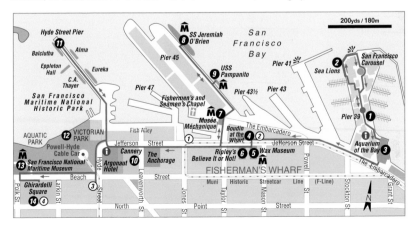

Traditional Dish

Cioppino is San Francisco's own brand of catch-of-the-day seafood stew. Its name is derived from *ciuppin,* meaning to chop in the Ligurian dialect spoken by the Italian fishermen who first created the dish out of San Francisco Bay's bounty; typically dungeness crab, clams, shrimp, scallops, squid, mussels, and fish with fresh tomatoes in a wine sauce.

Below: joggers near Pier 45.

com; June–Sept: daily 9am–11pm (Fri–Sat until midnight), Sept–May: daily 10am–10pm (Fri–Sat until midnight); charge), with its bizarre exhibits that include a cable-car model made of 270,836 matchsticks.

PIER 45

Turn right at Taylor Street to reach Pier 45, which along with nearby **Fish Alley** forms the working heart of Fisherman's Wharf. From here, fishermen depart in the before dawn and return midmorning. Their catch is packed and sold in the tin-roofed sheds along Fish Alley. The same fishermen often guide or captain the many bay tours that launch from here in the afternoon.

Musée Mécanique

At Pier 45's Shed A is the **Musée Mécanique** ❼ (tel: 346-2000; www.museemecanique.org; daily 10am–7pm, Sat–Sun until 8pm; free), an exercise in nostalgia with some 300 mechanical relics. Bring a pocket full

of change for vintage penny-arcade games, antique slot machines, hand-cranked music boxes, coin-operated pianos, and dubious fortune-tellers.

SS Jeremiah O'Brien

Further down Pier 45 is the **SS** *Jeremiah O'Brien* ❽ (tel: 544-0100; www.ssjeremiahobrien.org; daily 9am–4pm; charge), which can be fully explored, from the engine room to the flying bridge. The functional WWII Liberty Ship participated in the D-Day invasion of Normandy, carrying supplies and personnel across the English Channel. Just next to the SS *Jeremiah O'Brien* is the submarine **USS** *Pampanito* ❾ (tel: 775-1943; www.maritime.org; May–Oct: daily 9am–8pm; charge).

THE CANNERY

Return on Taylor Street and turn right on Jefferson Street. Just after the **Anchorage Hotel**, enter the redbrick **Cannery** ❿ (Jefferson and Leavenworth streets; tel: 771-3112; www.

delmontesquare.com; hours vary between businesses). The former Del Monte cannery (once the largest fruit and vegetable cannery in the world) is now a popular shopping center, filled with gourmet markets, piazzas for alfresco dining, and art galleries.

HYDE STREET PIER

Back on Jefferson Street, continue west and turn right on Hyde Street. The **Hyde Street Pier** ⓫ was the original Ferry terminal for Sausalito and Berkeley, and is home to the **Hyde Street Pier Historic Ships Collection** (tel: 447-5000; www.nps.gov/safr; daily 9.30am–5pm (call for extended summer hours); charge). The pier is part of the National Maritime Park, the country's smallest national park. Its Visitor Center is located across the street in the **Argonaut Hotel** (499 Jefferson Street; tel: 447-5000).

Moored along the pier are vintage vessels built in the late 19th and early 20th centuries. Tour below decks of the steam-driven *Eureka*, which was built in 1890 and ferried passengers between San Francisco and Tiburon before the bay's bridges were built. See how to set the topsail and staysail on board the *Balclutha*, a steel-hulled Scottish square-rigger built in 1886 that made 17 journeys around Cape Horn before its final voyage in 1930. Time your visit right and you can also raise your voice to the tune of sailor songs at the monthly Chantey Sing (tel: 561-7171; 1st Saturday of month; reservations required). The other his-

toric ships on site are two schooners, a steam tug, and a paddlewheel tug.

Walk south on Hyde Street toward Beach Street. You will pass **Victorian Park** ⓬ on the left, frequently filled with people waiting for the **Powell-Hyde cable-car** line that ends here. Just past Beach Street, break for a legendary Irish coffee at **Buena Vista Café**, see ⑪③.

AQUATIC PARK AND SAN FRANCISCO NATIONAL MARITIME MUSEUM

Walk west along Beach Street, overlooking **Aquatic Park** whose pleasant urban beach and romantic promenade lead to the **Municipal Pier** and on to **Fort Mason** *(see p.84)* one of the city's earliest military installations that dates back to the 1850s.

Perched above Aquatic Park is the **San Francisco National Maritime Museum** ⓭ (900 Beach Street; www. nps.gov/safr/ historyculture/maritime-museum.htm), re-opening in late 2009

Above from far left: Fort Mason Center; photographing the fish at the Aquarium of the Bay *(see p.29)*; Hyde Street Pier; the Art Deco National Maritime Museum.

Above: view of Fisherman's Wharf from the sea; sea captain sign at the National Maritime Museum.

Seamen's Chapel
Tucked away amid a network of piers and boats, the tiny Fishermen's and Seamen's Chapel is dedicated to those lost at sea in North California. Once a year, traditionally on the first Sunday of October, there is a ceremony blessing San Francisco's fishing fleet.

Food and Drink 🍴

③ BUENA VISTA CAFÉ
2765 Hyde Street; tel: 474-5044; www.thebuenavista.com; daily B, L, and D; $$
A San Francisco institution and home of the legendary Irish coffee, a delicious elixir made with Irish whiskey, frothed cream, and coffee. The recipe was whipped up in 1952 in response to a challenge made by writer Stan Delaplane, and is still served in steaming chalices to up to 2,000 happy drinkers each day.

Above from left: Ghirardelli's chocolate emporium; detail of a souvenir Alcatraz T-shirt; the former prison island of Alcatraz from above.

after renovations. Built during the 1930s with the rest of Aquatic Park, it resembles a beached ocean liner in the Art Deco style of its day. The museum celebrates San Francisco's colorful maritime heritage with interactive exhibits, intricate models, muralist Hilaire Hiler's 1930s expressionist vision of Atlantis, oral history recreations, and scores of other seafaring memorabilia, from tools to artifacts to photographs.

GHIRARDELLI SQUARE

Cross Beach Street to end your day at **Ghirardelli Square** ⑭ (900 North Point Street; tel: 775-5500; www.ghirardellisq.com), the proud recipient of city, state, and federal landmark status. A busy shopping center capped

Below: tempting ice-cream sign.

by a 15ft (4m) illuminated sign, Ghirardelli Square is named after Domingo Ghirardelli, an Italian merchant who settled in San Francisco in 1849 and opened the original Ghirardelli Chocolate Factory just 13 days before the gold discovery at Sutter's Mill that led to the Gold Rush. Focus on the dessert options here, especially the decadent sundaes at **Ghirardelli Chocolate Ice Cream and Chocolate Shop**, see ⑪④.

POWELL–HYDE CABLE-CAR

The tour ends here, but a great way to return downtown is via quintessential San Francisco transportation: the cable-car. Return to Larkin and Beach streets and then wait in line for the Powell–Hyde service, which runs through Russian Hill's leafy Hyde Street, over Nob Hill's hair-raising slopes, along the edge of Chinatown, and down to Union Square. The cable-cars generally depart every 10–20 minutes from 6am to 1am (at time of printing a single ticket was $5, an all-day pass $11).

Food and Drink 🍴

④ GHIRARDELLI
CHOCOLATE ICE CREAM
AND CHOCOLATE SHOP
Ghirardelli Square at Larkin; tel: 474-3938; www.ghirardelli.com; Sun–Thur 9am–11pm, Fri–Sat 9am–midnight; $
With a separate ice cream fountain that opens at 10am every day, this is a tried-and-true spot for ice cream, hot fudge, and all things scrumptiously chocolate.

ALCATRAZ

Hop on a ferry to explore the famous cell blocks of Alcatraz, the Disneyland of the world's former prison islands. Where once infamous criminals were incarcerated, the island now sees more than 1.4 million visitors each year and is the most visited attraction in San Francisco.

Tales of The Rock have fascinated Americans since the golden years of the American gangster. Now operated by the National Parks Service, anyone can come and go to Alcatraz not just to explore the prison, but also the island's unique flora and fauna.

Early History

Originally built as a military garrison, Alcatraz was prized for its strategic significance. It became a prison in 1895, when Modoc and Hopi tribe leaders

---

DISTANCE Less than 1 mile (2km)

TIME 3 hours

START/END Pier 33

POINTS TO NOTE

Book tickets in advance; tel: (information) 561-4926, (tickets) 981-7625; tours: www.alcatrazcruises.com; daily 9am (first ferry out), 4:30pm (last ferry back); charge; Metro: F to Embarcadero and Bay Street; bus: 10, 15.

What to Wear

Both the island and the ferry ride to it can be plagued by cold and foggy weather, regardless of the time of year. Wear layers and comfortable walking shoes to negotiate the uneven walkways and steep, uphill climb from the dock to the main level. For more information visit www.parksconservancy.org/visit/alcatraz/index.asp and www.nps.gov/alcatraz.

UNITED STATES PENITENTIARY

ALCATRAZ ISLAND | AREA 12 ACRES

$1\frac{1}{2}$ MILES TO TRANSPORT DOCK

ONLY GOVERNMENT BOATS PERMITTED

OTHERS MUST KEEP OFF 200 YARDS

NO ONE ALLOWED ASHORE

WITHOUT A PASS

Left: rules and regulations were once strictly enforced.

Prison Gardens

Recently, the Alcatraz Historic Gardens Project rebuilt the gardens and natural landscape surrounding the prison. Once tended by inmates and prison personnel as a popular pastime, these gardens provided color, as well as hope and reprieve from the harsh world behind the penitentiary's locked doors.

were imprisoned there. Responding to the crime wave sweeping the country in the 1920s and 1930s, the government decided Alcatraz was sufficiently fortified to house the most violent offenders, and took over the prison in 1934.

Federal Penitentiary

The cell blocks were once home to some of the most hardened criminals of the 20th century, including Chicago mob boss Al Capone, bootlegger George "Machine Gun" Kelly, and Robert Shroud (played by Burt Lancaster in the film *The Birdman of Alcatraz*). Alcatraz Federal Penitentiary quickly gained a reputation for its harsh system of earned privileges for the most basic rights, its deadening solitary confinement, and the cold, damp weather. Of 36 attempted escapes, none succeeded: of these 23 were caught alive, six were shot and killed during their escape, two drowned, and five were not found and presumed drowned. In 1963, Attorney General Robert

Kennedy closed the crumbling and expensive prison, and it was turned over to the National Park Service.

Indian Occupation

Six years later, a large group of Native Americans under the banner "Indians of All Tribes" occupied the island until 1971. Protesting against the many treaties with Native Americans that had been broken by the U.S. government, the group claimed Alcatraz as well as funds to build an Indian center and university. While the occupation ended with no demands met, it jumpstarted the Pan-Indian Movement and prompted the U.S. government to adopt a policy of Indian self-determination. Lasting reminders of the occupation include the burned-out shell of the warden's house destroyed by a 1970 fire, a blaze the group was unable to extinguish as the government had cut off their only water source a few weeks before.

VISITING THE PARK

A ferry service to the island departs from Pier 33, roughly every half-hour from 9am–1:55pm and takes about

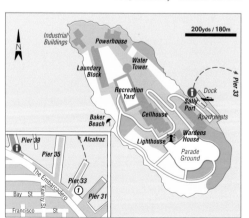

> ### Food and Drink 🍴
> **① EAGLE CAFÉ**
> Pier 39; tel: 433-3689; daily B, L, and D; $
> A great alternative to many higher-priced Fisherman's Wharf restaurants, the Eagle is a lively institution known for large portions, hearty breakfasts, stiff cocktails, and stellar views.

10–15 minutes each way; return ferries run until 4:30pm. It is advised to allow at least 2¹/₂ hours for the entire trip. Tickets (which can be purchased online, by phone, or at Pier 33) are pricey, but cover the transit cost and the 45-minute Cellhouse Audio Tour. Popular Night Tours are also available (Thur–Mon 4:30pm; charge), with a narrated boat tour around the island, guided island tours, and a variety of special activities. During the summer, on weekends, and holidays tickets should be purchased in advance.

On the Island

Somber by day and eerily illuminated at night, Alcatraz is a haunting presence in the bay. Once on the island, ask park rangers for assistance and information regarding tours. The cells and notorious Segregation Unit can be viewed; there is also a museum, two bookstores, and a visitor center located both on the dock and at the main level. Kid-friendly programs are available along with guided walks through the island's gardens and natural landscape, which offers a rare and unique variety of plant, animal, and bird life. Also note the island's lighthouse; built in 1854, it was the first lighthouse on the bay.

Back on the Mainland

Food is not available on the island, so bring refreshments or head to Pier 39 when you return for a bite at the **Eagle Café**, see ⒕①.

Above: until 1963 Alcatraz was home to some of the country's most hardened criminals.

Below: prison cell.

NORTH BEACH AND TELEGRAPH HILL

North Beach is a colorful, compact Italian neighborhood with restaurants, funky bars and cafés, bookstores, and strip joints. Neighboring Telegraph Hill offers stunning 360-degree views from its Coit Tower.

1906 Specials
In the 1906 earthquake, North Beach was totally destroyed. It was quickly rebuilt, but with few of the architectural flourishes for which the city is famous. These understated Victorian and Edwardian buildings came to be known as "1906 specials."

Below: Coit Tower and Telegraph Hill.

> **DISTANCE** 2 miles (3km)
> **TIME** A half-day
> **START** Jackson Square
> **END** Levi's Plaza
> **POINTS TO NOTE**
> Stairways render this tour from Coit Tower onwards inaccessible by wheelchair. The tour starts at Jackson Square, at Pacific and Montgomery (BART and Metro: Embarcadero and Montgomery stations; bus: 15, 30, 45).

Despite its name, North Beach borders no water, but was given its name at a time when the bay extended roughly to today's Bay Street. Tucked into the valley between Russian Hill and Telegraph Hill, the neighborhood is best-known for its excesses in literature, food, libations, and sex. It is where you can find the ghosts of the city's famed Beat past and the best espresso in the city, with the area's early-1900s Italian roots still much in evidence.

Telegraph Hill, which has always been a part of, and yet apart from, North Beach, was largely ignored by early settlers, who preferred to fill in the shallows of the bay below rather than build on the hill itself. Irish stevedores were some of the earliest inhabitants of the hill, using the rickety network of stairs to get to and from work and the docks every day. They were replaced by Italian immigrants, then later by bohemians, who liked the views and seclusion. Today, real estate around Telegraph Hill is among the most desirable in San Francisco.

NORTH BEACH

Start the tour at **Jackson Square ❶**, one of the best remaining enclaves of mid-

19th-century San Francisco. Built in the 1850s, the brick architecture that surrounds it withstood the 1906 earthquake and the following fire. Despite its chic galleries, antiques stores, design studios, and quaint, tree-lined ambience, this square was once the most notorious of the city's red light districts, and known as the "Barbary Coast."

Columbus Avenue

Walk west on Jackson Street and turn right onto Columbus Avenue. This intersection hosts the flatiron **Sentinel Building ②** at 916 Kearny Street, restored by film director and producer Francis Ford Coppola in the 1970s and now home to Coppola's production company, American Zoetrope Studios. Columbus is one of North Beach's dom-

inant commercial streets, filled with delis, restaurants, and cafés that spill onto the sidewalks. Another main thoroughfare is narrow Grant Avenue, home to family-run Italian businesses and the center of the North Beach social scene.

City Lights Bookstore

After World War II, rents in North Beach were low, the jazz and coffeehouse scenes lively, and the neighborhood's character lascivious; the area became the West Coast hub of Beat poets, writers, and artists. Among them were Jack Kerouac, Allen Ginsberg, Gary Snyder, Lawrence Ferlinghetti, Philip Whalen, and Michael McClure. This heritage is still visible at **City Lights Bookstore ③** (261 Columbus Avenue; tel: 362-8193; www.citylights.

Above from far left: elegant mansion on Jackson Square; chilling at Mario's Bohemian Cigar Store (see p.38); bookworm's delight and Beatnik haunt, City Lights Bookstore.

Above: local attractions include City Lights bookstore (top) and the Vesuvio Cafe (middle); a warm welcome at a strip club.

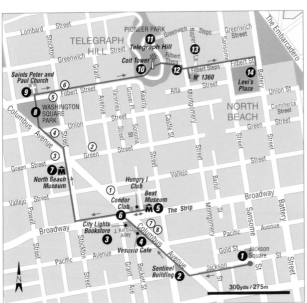

com; daily 10am–midnight) a left-leaning "Beatnikdom" cornerstone that was co-founded by Ferlinghetti and is now a National Literary Landmark. Also a publisher, City Lights gained notoriety in 1956 by publishing Allen Ginsburg's poem *Howl* and winning the obscenity case that was brought against the company.

Vesuvio Cafe

Next door to City Lights sits **Vesuvio Cafe ❹** (255 Columbus Avenue; tel: 362-3370; www.vesuvio.com; daily 6am–2am), a cool Beatnik haunt frequented by everyone from Bob Dylan to Dylan Thomas. Here, Jack Kerouac

was famously "delayed" one night in 1960 when he was scheduled to meet novelist Henry Miller in Big Sur. Between Vesuvio and City Lights is **Jack Kerouac Alley**, one of several city streets honoring local literati. The truly Beat-obsessed can turn right at Broadway for the **Beat Museum ❺** (540 Broadway Street; tel: 800-537-6822; www.thebeatmuseum.org; daily 10am–10pm; charge), which displays a handful of books, photographs, letters, and other memorabilia and hosts occasional events such as film screenings.

At Grant and Vallejo, stop at the West Coast's home of the espresso, **Caffe Trieste**, see ⑪①. This was another Beatnik hang and allegedly where Coppola wrote his screenplay for *The Godfather*.

Red-Light District

The **intersection of Columbus, Broadway and Grant ❻** gamely carries on the Barbary Coast's red-light tradition. Today, it is jam-packed with strip-clubs, adult video parlors, and racy late-night clubs, including the **Hungry I** (546 Broadway Street), which helped launch the careers of big names such as Wood Allen and Bill Cosby. Carol Doda made history at the **Condor Club** (300 Columbus Avenue) performing the first topless (1964) then bottomless (1969) act in the country, while descending from the ceiling on top of a piano. For years, Ms. Doda's three-story likeness – complete with red neon nipples – loomed over the sidewalk on the corner of Broadway and Columbus.

Food and Drink 🍴

① CAFFE TRIESTE
601 Vallejo Street; tel: 392-6739; www.caffetrieste.com; daily 6.30am–11pm (Fri–Sat until midnight); $
Serious about its espresso, this casual, family-run and quintessentially San Francisco coffeehouse claims to be the first place on the West Coast to serve espresso back in the 1950s. Cash only.

② GOLDEN BOY PIZZA
542 Green Street; tel: 982-9738; daily L and D; $
Golden Boy's Sicilian-style pan pizza is a favorite of North Beach bar-goers, and usually ordered by the slice. Look in the window and choose what whets the appetite.

③ L'OSTERIA DEL FORNO
519 Columbus Avenue; tel: 982-1124; daily L and D; $ (cash only)
Come for casual but satisfying Italian food, including marvelous antipasti, thin-crusted pizzas, a daily-changing pasta special, and a fine roast pork loin simmered in a milk broth. This treasure is a kid-pleaser as well.

④ MARIO'S BOHEMIAN CIGAR STORE
566 Columbus Avenue; tel: 362-0536; daily 10am–11pm; $
Cigars are not on the menu of this tiny slice of a café, but you can find a killer cappuccino along with delicious small pizzas, baked focaccia sandwiches, beer, and wine.

North Beach Museum

Turn west on Stockton Street, where tucked away in a bank building, the **North Beach Museum** ❼ (1435 Stockton Street; Mon–Fri 9am–4pm; free) celebrates the history and culture of the vibrant North Beach neighborhood with artifacts and vintage photographs. Several excellent espresso and lunch options are in the vicinity, see ⑪②, ⑪③, and ⑪④.

Washington Square

Continue along Columbus to escape from North Beach's congested streets into **Washington Square Park** ❽, where a rainbow of types – elderly Italians, Chinese tai chi devotees, sunbathers, and Frisbee-tossers – makes for prime people-watching. The life-sized Ben Franklin statue dates from 1879 and is the oldest existing monument in San Francisco.

Saints Peter and Paul Church

Across Filbert Street are the picturesque Romanesque façade and soaring twin white spires of **Saints Peter and Paul Church** ❾ (666 Filbert Street; tel: 421-0809; www.stspeterpaul.san-francisco.ca.us/church; daily 7am–4pm (Sat–Sun until 6pm); free). Built in 1924, the Catholic church holds Mass each day in Italian, Chinese, and English, and is popular for traditional Italian weddings. Baseball legend Joe DiMaggio and his bride Marilyn Monroe even snapped photos here, although their ceremony was held at City Hall. The church's many silver-screen credits include Cecil B.

DeMille's *The Ten Commandments* (1956) and Don Siegel's *Dirty Harry* (1971). Above the main entrance is an inscription from Dante's *Paradiso*.

Before climbing Telegraph Hill, have brunch at **Mama's**, see ⑪⑤ *(see p.40)* or grab perhaps the city's best focaccia at the **Liguria Bakery**, see ⑪⑥ *(see p.40)*.

Below: Saints Peter and Paul Church.

TELEGRAPH HILL

Those with dwindling energy can catch the 39 bus to reach **Coit Tower** ❿ (Telegraph Hill Boulevard; tel: 362-0808; daily 10am–6.30pm; charge). Others can climb Filbert Street to the east to reach the 210ft (64m) landmark. Surrounded by Pioneer Park, Coit Tower crowns **Telegraph Hill** ⓫, so named in 1849 when it became the site of the first telegraph on the West Coast. The tower whose exterior resembles a fire-hose nozzle is a monument to city firefighters, and was erected in 1933 at the bequest of volunteer firefighter and North Beach eccentric, Lillie Hitchcock Coit. Inside are murals in the style of the Mexican artist Diego Rivera, and dazzling 360-degree views can be enjoyed from the top.

Filbert Steps and Napier Lane

Outside, look for the **Filbert Steps** ⓬ to the right (on the left are the **Greenwich Steps**) and descend the wooden staircases surrounded by cool, shady gardens. When you reach Montgomery Street, detour to the right briefly to see **1360 Montgomery**, a four-story Art Deco building that starred in the Humphrey Bogart film *Dark Passage* (1947). Continue down the Filbert Steps, passing **Napier Lane** ⓭ on the left, the last wooden plank street left in the city. Listen for the famous flock of wild Red-headed conures, whose fame has spread since the 2000 documentary "The Wild Parrots of Telegraph Hill."

Levi's Plaza

From Filbert Street turn right on Battery Street to head back to North Beach; continue until you reach the red bricks and grassy knolls of **Levi's Plaza** ⓮, home of the headquarters of the blue jeans experts Levi Strauss.

If you finish the tour at the end of the day, head south along Battery, then turn right on Broadway to return to the heart of North Beach for drinks at an historic watering hole. As well as Vesuvio Cafe *(see p.38)*, **Tosca** and **Specs 12 Adler Museum Café**, see ⑪⑦ and ⑪⑧, are good choices.

Food and Drink

⑤ MAMA'S
1701 Stockton Street; tel: 362-6421; www.mamas-sf.com; Tue–Sun B and L; $
A legendary brunch spot; the line is crazy on weekends, so bring a cup of coffee or try going during the week. Generous egg dishes, stacks of pancakes, and Monte Cristo sandwiches are among the offerings at this atmospheric local favorite.

⑥ LIGURIA BAKERY
1700 Stockton Street; tel: 421-3786; Mon–Fri 8am–2pm, Sat 7am–2pm, Sun 7am–noon (closes earlier if they sell out); $
This is one for early birds only. Available in just a few flavors (including raisin, garlic, rosemary, and black olive), the melt-in-your-mouth bread drips with olive oil and sells out quickly. Cash only.

⑦ TOSCA
242 Columbus Avenue; tel: 986-9651; daily 5pm–2am; no food
The classy 1940s-style Tosca is a San Francisco institution, pulling in celebrities, self-styled bohemians, yuppies and movie cameras (eg for *Basic Instinct*) to its red vinyl booths and long bar. The writer Hunter S. Thompson broke his arm here, pirouetting off the bar.

⑧ SPECS 12 ADLER MUSEUM CAFÉ
12 William Saroyan Place; tel: 421-4112; Mon–Fri 5pm–2am; $
This friendly, characterful dive bar is where seamen have donated salty trinkets from their adventures since the 1940s. For food, crackers and cheese are all that's on offer. Cash only.

CHINATOWN

Amble through Chinatown's animated streets and alleys, which buzz with commotion and are peppered with produce stands, purveyors of fortune cookies, tiny temples, dried herbs, dim sum, and swarms of souvenirs.

San Francisco's Chinatown is one of those rare tourist attractions that is also a dynamic community. It is as close as you can get to a city within a city, complete with its own banks, schools, doctors, video stores, and sweatshops, sadly reminiscent of those at the turn of the 20th century.

Historic Hub

Despite Chinatown's being in a sense a world of its own, it has been a significant part of San Francisco's history since the earliest days of the Gold Rush. Due to the political upheaval and widespread famine in Southern China in the 1850s, thousands of Chinese came to California to find their fortunes in the goldfields of the Sierras or to work on the Transcontinental Railroad. These immigrants quickly set up a commercial district near the then center of town, Portsmouth Square.

By the mid-19th century, "Little Canton," as it was then known, was filled with hotels, boarding houses, restaurants, stores, and pharmacies plying herbal remedies. Christened "Chinatown" by the local press, it was also notorious as a den of vice. Brothels, opium dens, and gambling rings were legion and often exaggerated to justify rampant anti-Chinese racism.

DISTANCE 1 mile (2km)
TIME 3 hours
START/END Chinatown Gate
POINTS TO NOTE
Visit during normal business hours when the streets are most alive. This route begins at the intersection of Bush Street and Grant Avenue near Union Square (BART and Metro: Montgomery or Powell Street stations; bus: Market Street lines).

Below: decorative street lamp on Grant Avenue.

Customer Service

In operation from 1894–1949, the Chinese Telephone Exchange was staffed by astonishingly capable female telephone operators. They not only spoke English and five Chinese dialects, but also memorized all the customers' names, as it was considered rude to refer to a person as a number. Moreover, they distinguished between people with the same name by memorizing addresses and job titles!

Discrimination and hostility reached a boiling point in the aftermath of the 1906 earthquake and fire, which leveled the ramshackle Chinatown. Seeing the opportunity to seize the valuable downtown real estate, as well as to eradicate what they saw as a blight on the city, San Francisco's leaders attempted to relocate Chinatown to the distant southeast corner of the city. However, the residents of Chinatown would have no such thing, and due to their steadfastness and the intervention of the Dowager Empress on behalf of her distant subjects, Chinatown was rebuilt in its original spot in the heart of the city. In recent years, the city's Chinese population has grown substantially in other areas including the Richmond, Sunset and

Russian Hill neighborhoods. Yet, with 75,000 residents packed into just 24 square blocks, Chinatown remains the thriving cultural heart of the Bay Area's Chinese community.

CHINATOWN GATE AND GRANT AVENUE

The "official" entrance of Chinatown is through the ornate **Chinatown Gate ❶** that arches over Grant Avenue. Gifted by Taiwan in 1970, the green, dragon-crested structure was modeled after a traditional village gate. Together with Bush Street, it marks the southern edge of Chinatown; the western, northern, and eastern borders are marked by Powell, Broadway, and Kearny streets, respectively.

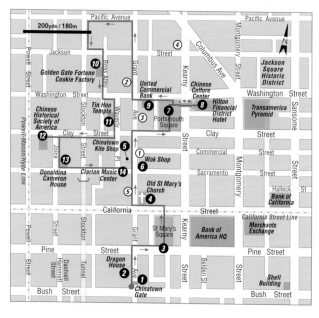

Pass underneath the gate along Grant Avenue, one of Chinatown's most vital arteries. Racks of tourist-targeting merchandise spill onto the sidewalks that are cluttered with silks and satiny slippers, teapots, and carved teak, jade, and jewelry, and other Chinese tchotchkes (souvenirs or knick-knacks).

Dragon House

A respite is offered by the authentic **Dragon House** ❷ (455 Grant Avenue; tel: 415-421-3693; daily 10am–6pm) and its genuine Asian antiques and fine arts. Though Grant Avenue feels in many ways like a Disney version of "Chinatown," do not be fooled: behind the tourist-oriented commercialism exists a thriving, insular, and in many ways impenetrable community.

ST MARY'S SQUARE

From Grant Avenue, turn right onto Pine Street. The entrance to **St Mary's Square** ❸ (daily 6am–10pm) is on the left. In this peaceful, prettily landscaped patch of green, Chinatown residents stroll winding paths and rest on wooden benches while children play. Note the large metal-and-granite statue designed by Beniamino Bufano; the statue honors reformer Dr. Sun Yat-sen, a leader of the rebellion that ended the Qing Dynasty's reign and helped to establish the Republic of China in the early 1900s.

OLD ST MARY'S CHURCH

Exit the square heading north and cross California Street to reach the Roman Catholic **Old St. Mary's Church** ❹ (660 California Street; tel: 288-3800; www.oldsaintmarys.org; Mon–Fri 7am–4:30pm, Sat 7am–6pm, Sun 7am–3pm; free). Established in 1853, this Paulist-led parish church was California's first cathedral and San Francisco's Catholic cathedral for most of the second half of the 19th century. Eventually its location amidst neighbors of ill repute (note the inscription outside beneath the clock that reads "Son Observe the Time and Fly from Evil") led to the construction of a new cathedral at a better-respected address. Although the building survived the 1906 earthquake, it was gutted by the ensuing fire and rebuilt in 1909.

NICHE SHOPS

Turn right onto Grant Avenue and continue north for some of Chinatown's unique shops. (If you need a pitstop at this point, pop into the **Eastern Bakery**, see ⑪①, at No. 720.) The **Chinatown Kite Shop** ❺ (717 Grant Avenue; tel: 989-5182; www.chinatownkite.com; daily 9:30am–9pm) is a kaleidoscope of kites in every

---

Above from far left: statue of Dr. Sun Yat-sen; Old St. Mary's; dragon on the Chinatown Gate.

Historic Street
Grant Avenue is the oldest street in San Francisco. First named in 1845 by the town of Yerba Buena as Calle de la Fundación, it also served a long stint as Dupont Street, in honor of an admiral of the U.S.S. *Portsmouth*.

Food and Drink

① EASTERN BAKERY
720 Grant Avenue; tel: 433-7973; www.easternbakery.com; daily B, L, and D; $
Billed as the oldest Chinese bakery in the U.S. (it opened in 1924), this slightly shabby spot is good for a quick pork bun or some traditional chinese pastries called mooncakes.

Chinese New Year
Every year in early spring, Chinatown sees the biggest Chinese New Year's celebration outside of Asia, cramming thousands into the neighborhood for festivities. Firecracker wrappers litter every alleyway, vendors fill the streets, and a spectacular parade with a 201ft (61m) Golden Dragon is the high point of the celebration.

Below: eating dim sum.

shape and size and is crammed with phoenixes, dragons, butterflies, and more. Across the street, the **Wok Shop** ➏ (716 Grant Avenue; tel: 989-3797; www.wokshop.com; daily 10am–6pm) dispenses woks, soup spoons, sake cups, and a melting pot of everything else you could want for Chinese cooking adventures.

PORTSMOUTH SQUARE

From Grant Avenue, turn right onto Clay Street to reach **Portsmouth Square ➐**. Designed in 1839, this Chinatown community gathering place is steeped in history and often considered the birthplace of San Francisco. The square was once the town center of Yerba Buena, and overlooked Yerba Buena Cove to the east, where the

Financial District skyscrapers stand today. In 1846, this was where Captain John Montgomery of the U.S.S. *Portsmouth* first raised the American flag, and a year later, it was the site of San Francisco's first school (a memorial in the square commemorates the event). Here also Sam Brannan, owner of San Francisco's first newspaper, the *California Star*, announced that gold had been discovered in the Sierra foothills.

Note the 600lb (272kg) bronze *Goddess of Democracy* statue created by volunteers led by sculptor Thomas Marsh. This is a smaller replica of the statue created during the Tiananmen Square protests of 1989.

In the northwest corner of the square is a tribute to writer Robert Louis Stevenson designed by Bruce Porter. In 1879–80, Stevenson came here to

ship-watch while waiting for his darling to divorce; today, idlers still flock to chat and people-watch, as youngsters clamber on jungle gyms and old men argue about politics while playing checkers and mah-jong at small tables that dot the square.

CULTURE CENTER

Use the short pedestrian bridge on the eastern edge of the square to enter the **Chinese Culture Center** ❸ (3rd floor; 750 Kearny Street, tel: 986-1822; www.c-c-c.org; Tue–Sat 10am–4pm; free) inside the Hilton San Francisco Financial District. This non-profit organization teaches about historical and modern practices and celebrations in Chinese and Chinese-American culture. Retrace your steps along the pedestrian bridge and exit the square on the north onto Washington Street.

UNITED COMMERCIAL BANK

Head west on Washington Street. On the left is one of Chinatown's original buildings, the **United Commercial Bank** ❾ (743 Washington Street; tel: 421-5215; Mon–Thur 9am–5pm, Fri 9am–6pm, Sat 9am–4pm; free). The three-tiered, pagoda-like structure was built in 1909 after the original was destroyed in the 1906 earthquake, and housed the Pacific Telephone and Telegraph Company's Chinese Telephone Exchange. California's first newspaper, the *California Star*, was also once printed here.

TOWARDS STOCKTON STREET

Turn north at Grant and continue until Broadway, taking time for a bite to eat at one of the several local options, see ⑪②, ⑪③, and ⑪④. Then check out where locals stock up for dinner by walking up Pacific Avenue and then turning left onto bustling **Stockton Street**. This is Chinatown's working center, crammed with Chinese-owned and operated businesses, countless dollar stores, and open-air fresh produce stands and markets.

GOLDEN GATE FORTUNE COOKIE FACTORY

Follow the scent of fresh fortune cookies and turn left onto Jackson Street and then right into the tiny

Food and Drink

② GOLDEN GATE BAKERY
1029 Grant Avenue; tel: 781-2627; daily B, L, and D; $
Beloved of locals, this bakery keeps the crowds happy with traditional treats like the egg custards that everyone raves about.

③ EMPRESS OF CHINA
838 Grant Avenue; tel: 434-1345; daily L and D; $
The only restaurant in Chinatown with a truly spectacular view gives diners a very good perspective on the neighborhood. The cocktail lounge overlooks Grant Street, while the dining room towers above Portsmouth Square. If you do not eat here, at least stop by for a drink and enjoy the ambience.

④ HOUSE OF NANKING
919 Kearny street; tel: 421-1429; daily L and D; $
Grungy and crowded, the reason for the lengthy line at nearly all hours is because this wildly popular spot is a neighborhood favorite and serves inexpensive yet outstanding and adventurous Chinese food. Take the advice of the no-nonsense owners and staff on what to order, and avoid weekends.

Above from left:
Waverly Place the "Street of Painted Balconies"; offerings at the Tin Hou Temple; buildings in the financial district of Union Square; cardboard cut-out of Bart Simpson at the Cartoon Art Museum.

Above: Chinese characters on flags in Grant Avenue (see p.42).

Ross Alley, where the **Golden Gate Fortune Cookie Factory** ❿ (56 Ross Alley; tel: 781-3956; daily 8am–8pm; free, small charge for taking photographs) has been producing cookie-encased predictions and words of wisdom since 1962. Watch the two workers take flat rounds off the press, stick a fortune inside, and fold them over a rod. Then taste some novelty flat and fortune-less cookies, bags of which are also for sale.

TIN HOU TEMPLE

Continue south on Ross and cross Washington Street to enter **Waverly Place**, an alley that may sound familiar to fans of Amy Tan's Chinatown-set *The Joy Luck Club*. Known as the "Street of Painted Balconies," Waverly offers a brief reprieve from Chinatown's frenetic hum, with stores selling "real" Chinese goodies: lychee wine, pickled ginger, and herbal remedies. At No. 125, climb up three floors to reach the historic **Tin Hou Temple** ⓫ (daily 10am–4pm; donation suggested), believed to be the oldest Chinese temple in the country. Red paper lanterns blanket the ceiling and incense fills the air inside this tiny

temple dedicated to the Queen of the Heavens and Goddess of the Seven Seas, a protector of travelers, sailors, artists, and prostitutes.

CHINESE HISTORICAL SOCIETY OF AMERICA

At the junction of Waverly Place and Clay Street, turn right to visit the **Chinese Historical Society of America** ⓬ (965 Clay Street; tel: 391-1188; www.chsa. org; Tue–Fri noon–5pm, Sat 11am–4pm; charge, 1st Thur of month free). At this museum and learning center, small displays explore Chinese-American history, art, and culture, including how Chinese contributions fueled the development of industries in the American West. Note that there is a wheelchair-accessible entrance on Joice Street.

BACK TO CHINATOWN GATE

Walk south on Joice, noting the dark, clinker-brick building on the corner at 920 Sacramento Street. It is the **Donaldina Cameron House** ⓭, designed by the notable San Francisco-born architect Julia Morgan (1872–1957). At this point turn left on Sacramento to browse Chinese and world musical instruments at **Clarion Music Center** ⓮ (816 Sacramento Street; tel: 391-1317; www.clarion music.com; Mon–Fri 11am–6pm, Sat 9am–5pm). Then turn right on Grant, passing **Far East Café**, see ⓫⑤, on your return to Chinatown Gate.

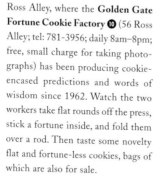

Food and Drink 🍴

⑤ **FAR EAST CAFÉ**
631 Grant Avenue; tel: 982-3245; daily L and D; $
The food here is good if not amazing, but the atmosphere is one of the best in Chinatown with private booths and century-old chandeliers.

SOUTH OF MARKET AND UNION SQUARE

Pick and choose from a smorgasbord of museums and shops on this downtown walk. There's everything from modern art, cartoon art, and historical museums to designer outposts and massive department stores.

Begin this tour on Mission Street between Second and Third streets, in the South of Market neighborhood. Once better-known as "South of the Slot" and, in more recent years, increasingly as SoMa, South of Market is a sprawling district with wide traffic-filled streets stacked with tall office buildings, condo highrises, hotels, nightclubs, and major museums. Three blocks north of Market Street is Union Square, the heart of the eponymous district famous for upscale stores and topend hotels.

CARTOON ART MUSEUM

Endowed by *Peanuts* cartoon-strip creator Charles M. Schulz, the **Cartoon Art Museum ❶** (655 Mission Street; tel: 227-8666; www.cartoonart.org; Tue–Sun 11am–5pm; charge, 1st Tue of month is "Pay What You Wish Day") showcases original cartoons and animation art of both underground and mainstream varieties. Rotating exhibits draw from a permanent collection of 6,000 pieces that range from graphic novels and comic strips to political and advertising cartoons.

DISTANCE 2 miles (3km)
TIME A half-day (or more depending on number of museums visited)
START Cartoon Art Museum
END Westfield San Francisco Shopping Centre
POINTS TO NOTE
It is not intended for you to visit all the museums on this walk (to do so would be exhausting), so choose a few that particularly catch your interest. This tour begins in the South of Market (SoMa) neighborhood (BART and Metro: Montgomery Street station; bus: 14, 30, 45, Market Street routes).

Extended Hours
On the first Tuesday of the month, many museums offer free admission. On the first Thursday of each month, the San Francisco tradition of "First Thursdays" turns typically calm galleries into lively, wine-sipping social events. Many galleries schedule their show openings and then keep their door open later than usual.

Below: detail from *Peanuts*, at the Cartoon Art Museum.

Above from left:
looking at Jasper
Johns's take on the
American flag *(left)* and
inside the foyer *(right)*,
at SFMOMA.

MUSEUM OF THE AFRICAN DIASPORA (MOAD)

Walk southeast toward Third Street along Mission street to reach the **Museum of the African Diaspora (MoAD) ❷** (685 Mission Street; tel: 358-7200; www.moadsf.org; Wed–Sat 11am–6pm, Sun noon–5pm; charge). The artwork and artifacts on exhibit focus on the global, uniting influence of the art, culture, and history of Africa. Permanent displays showcase rituals and ceremony, slavery passages, music, theater, adornment, and culinary traditions, and are supplemented with varied rotating exhibits.

CALIFORNIA HISTORICAL SOCIETY

Just across the street from MoAD is the **California Historical Society Museum ❸** (678 Mission Street; tel: 357-1848; www.californiahistorical society.org; Wed–Sat noon–4.30pm; charge). In this museum, early California history is chronicled by 5,000 oil paintings, drawings, costumes, lithographs, and decorative arts. There is also an important collection of 500,000 photographs, including works by Eadweard Muybridge and Ansel Adams, and a good gift shop, selling books and souvenirs.

SAN FRANCISCO MUSEUM OF MODERN ART (SFMOMA)

Turn left on Third Street to reach the **San Francisco Museum of Modern Art ❹** (151 Third Street; tel: 357-4000; www.sfmoma.org; Thur 11am–8:45pm, Fri–Tue 11am–5:45pm; daily from 10am in summer); charge except Thur 6–9pm and 1st Tue of month). The SFMOMA celebrated its 60th anniversary in 1995 by moving into a striking new South of Market location. The building – marked by a truncated tower with black-and-white bands – was designed by internationally renowned Swiss architect Mario Botta.

Inside, natural light pours into the airy atrium and four floors of galleries that display a permanent collection strong in American Abstract Expressionism, Fauvism, and German Expressionism. Be sure to see Henri Matisse's seminal *Femme au chapeau (Woman with the Hat)*, painted in 1905. Other painting highlights include Jackson Pollock's *Guardians of the Secret* (1943), René Magritte's 1952 *Les Valeurs personnelles (Personal Values)*, and works by Paul Klee, Piet Mondrian, Pablo Picasso, Andy Warhol, and Georgia O'Keeffe. Diego Rivera's bold, bright *Cargador de flores (The Flower Carrier*, 1935) is complemented by Frida Kahlo's *Frida y Diego Rivera* (1931).

Also look for Marcel Duchamp's uproar-igniting *Fountain*, his most famous ready-made work. This glazed ceramic urinal is a replica Duchamp created in 1964; the 1917 original was lost. The fine photography collection includes works by Alfred Stieglitz, Edward Weston, Ansel Adams, Dorthea Lange, Robert Frank, and William Klein. In the museum store you will find cutting-edge design objects and contemporary art books, while the Mediterranean-style menu of **Caffe Museo**, see ⑪①, makes this a popular lunch stop.

YERBA BUENA GARDENS

Cross Third Street into the lovely **Yerba Buena Gardens ❺** (www.yerba

Food and Drink 🍴

① CAFFE MUSEO
151 Third Street; tel: 357-4500; www.caffemuseo.com; Thur 10am–9pm, Fri–Tue 10am–6pm; $$
Accessible from the street, SFMOMA's relaxed café is a destination in its own right. Stylish and airy, with plenty of sidewalk seating, it serves up coffee, beer, wine, and light café food.

Below: window of the Museum of the African Diaspora.

Above: electric ukulele, Museum of Craft and Folk Art; Maiden Lane; child's play at the Zeum.

Vive la France!
To the northeast of Union Square is the little-known French Quarter of San Francisco. Alleyways such as Belden Place and Claude Alley are full of French bistros and cafés and are particularly lively each year on Bastille Day (July 14). Here you can enjoy French bistro fare, alluring accents, and a casual, romantic ambience with outside seating, see ⑪②.

buenagardens.com; Mon–Sun 6am–10pm; free), an urban oasis featuring grassy landscaping, fountains, cafés, public artwork, and a waterfall memorial to Dr. Martin Luther King, Jr. On the southwest corner is the Metreon (tel: 369-6201; www.westfield.com/metreon) an entertainment complex with some 15 theaters, a giant Imax screen, shops, and restaurants, which really comes into its own on rainy days.

Located in a two-building complex, the **Yerba Buena Center for the Arts** ❻ (YBCA, 701 Mission Street; tel: 978-2787; www.ybca.org; gallery hours: Tue–Wed, Fri–Sun noon–5pm, Thur noon–8pm; charge except 1st Tue of month) exhibits contemporary art along with community-based work and also presents contemporary dance, theater, music, and cross-disciplinary performances from both national and international performers.

One block south, and very much geared towards children, is **Zeum** ❼ (221 Fourth Street; tel: 820-3320; www.zeum.org; Wed–Fri 1–5pm, Sat–Sun 11am–5pm, call for longer summer hours; charge). Among the attractions here are an ice-skating rink, bowling center, and carrousel (daily 11am–6pm), as well as Zeum itself: a hands-on multimedia arts and technology museum that teaches children about animation, digital technology, and electronic media and helps them create movies, music, and art.

SOCIETY OF CALIFORNIA PIONEERS MUSEUM

Exit Yerba Buena Gardens onto Fourth Street to reach the **Society of California Pioneers Museum** ❽ (300 Fourth Street; tel: 957-1849; www.californiapioneers.org; Wed–Fri 10am–4pm, 1st Sat of month 10am–4pm; free). This is home to a sizeable collection of paintings, photographs, works on paper, silverware, and mining artifacts that vividly chronicle California history from the Gold Rush era to the 1940s.

CONTEMPORARY JEWISH MUSEUM

At this point in the tour, make your way back through Yerba Buena Gardens, exiting onto Mission Street to reach the **Contemporary Jewish Museum** ❾ (736 Mission Street; tel: 344-8800; www.thecjm.org; Fri–Tue 11am–5.30pm, Thur 1–8:30pm; charge), which focuses on Jewish art and culture. The new facility designed by architect Daniel Libeskind – also responsible for New York City's Freedom Tower – incorporates the historic Jessie Street Power Substation.

Food and Drink 🍴

② PLOUF
40 Belden Place; tel: 986-6491;
Mon–Fri L and D, Sat D only; $$$
One of several good café-restaurants with outdoor seating on the charming Belden Place alleyway. Plouf specializes in delicious seafood with a French accent. The French waiters also give the impression that you have arrived in the Paris of the West.

MUSEUM OF CRAFT AND FOLK ART

Exit the museum and turn right to find the charming pedestrian **Yerba Buena Lane**, a quiet enclave of stores and cafés. Also here is the **Museum of Craft and Folk Art ⑩** (51 Yerba Buena Lane; tel: 227-4888; www. mocfa.org; Tue–Fri 11am–6pm, Sat–Sun 11am–5pm; charge), which exhibits traditional and contemporary craft and folk art from all over the world.

49 GEARY STREET

Exit Yerba Buena Lane onto Market Street and cross onto Grant Avenue. Then turn right on Geary Street to reach the high-rise at **49 Geary Street ⑪**, a particularly popular art gallery address that houses the renowned **Fraenkel Gallery** among others. The cluster of galleries around Union Square is the city's thickest (several more galleries are found on nearby Sutter Street). For a handy guide of maps, addresses, and details on specific events, pick up a copy of the *Art Now Gallery Guide – West Coast* or *San Francisco Bay Area Gallery Guide* in any gallery. Both publications are free.

MAIDEN LANE

Now turn left off Geary onto Kearny Street. For a detour the French Quarter's Belden Place *(see margin tip, left)*, head north to Bush Street and turn right. Otherwise, turn left on **Maiden Lane ⑫**. This pedestrian-only street is top-notch real estate,

Above from far left: Zeum; old-fashioned merry-go-round in the Yerba Buena Gardens; artwork at the Museum of Craft and Folk Art; SFMOMA art: furniture on the exterior of a building.

Maiden Lane

Maiden Lane's tongue-in-cheek name originated from its notorious red-light past during the city's rowdy "Barbary Coast" days. Then the lane was called Morton Street and was known for having the cheapest prostitutes in town. When the brothels burned down in the 1906 fire, Maiden Lane rose from the ashes. Today the two cool, shaded blocks conduct anything but shady business: they are studded with glossy boutiques such as Chanel and Diptyche, along with sumptuous San Francisco institution Gump's and seamstress seventh heaven Britex Fabrics.

Above from left:
Union Square; Victory
statue; City Hall
dome; boy reading
in the Manga Room,
Asian Art Museum.

What's in a Name?
Union Square is as old
as San Francisco itself.
First deeded for public
use in 1850, it got its
name a decade later
when it was used to
rally support for the
Union cause during
the Civil War.

filled with classy shops. At No. 140 is
the **Xanadu Gallery** ⑬ (tel: 392-9999;
www.folkartintl.com; Tue–Sat 10am–
6pm; free), a collection of artwork, textiles, jewelry, and artifacts from around
the world that is located in the city's
only building designed by architect
Frank Lloyd Wright.

UNION SQUARE

At the end of Maiden Lane, cross
Stockton Street into **Union Square** ⑭,
where the city's shopping pulse thumps

most wildly. The streets are stacked
with elegant emporia including **Saks
Fifth Avenue**, **Neiman Marcus**, and
Macy's, and accompanied by an A-list
roster of international luxury retailers,
from Cartier to Hermès. Redesigned in
2002, Union Square is sleek and
modern, and provides a place of repose
for the weary shopper. At the square's
center is a 90ft (27m) Corinthian
column topped by a bronze Victory
commemorating the successful Manila
Bay campaign during the Spanish-
American War of 1898.

To have a break from shopping, stop
for French bistro fare at **Café de la
Presse**, see ⑪③, a hearty meal at
Sears Fine Food, see ⑪④, cocktails at
the **Redwood Room**, see ⑪⑤, or wine
at **The Hidden Vine**, see ⑪⑥.

WESTFIELD SAN FRANCISCO SHOPPING CENTRE

From Union Square, head south on
Powell to Market Street, past the cable-
car terminus of the Powell–Hyde and
Powell–Mason routes. The stairway on
the right descends to the **San Francisco Visitor Center**. Cross Market for
the **Westfield San Francisco Shopping Centre** ⑮ (865 Market Street;
tel: 512-6776; http://westfield.com/
uscentres; Mon–Sat 9:30am–9pm, Sun
10am–7pm), an indoor mall with
unusual escalators that spiral around a
nine-story atrium, whisking shoppers
to **Nordstrom** at the top. There is also
an upmarket **Bloomingdales** and a
large downstairs food court.

Food and Drink

③ CAFÉ DE LA PRESSE
352 Grant Avenue; tel: 398-2680; www.aqua-sf.com;
daily B, L, and D; $$
Join the European literati at the tables that spill out onto the
sidewalk at this charming French café. Dine on sandwiches,
Alsatian tarts, and other classic French bistro fare, washed
down with espresso shots and glasses of beer and wine.
Inside, international magazines and newspapers are for sale.

④ SEARS FINE FOOD
439 Powell Street; tel: 986-0700; daily B, L, and D; $$
The Swedish pancakes are legendary here, but this diner now
boasts an extended and tasty menu for brunch (until 3pm each
day) and beyond.

⑤ REDWOOD ROOM AT THE CLIFT HOTEL
495 Geary Street; tel: 982-6168; www.clifthotel.com; Sun–Thur
5pm–2am, Fri–Sat 4pm–2am; drinks only
Legend has it that this historic San Francisco hotel bar was
carved from a single redwood tree. Recently redesigned by
Philippe Starck, it still retains its elegance, but now with a
modern twist. Alternatively, join the young, well-heeled crowd
sipping cocktails in the bar of the Clift's Asia de Cuba restaurant.

⑥ THE HIDDEN VINE
½ Cosmo Place (off Taylor); tel: 674-3567; www.thehidden
vine.com; Tue–Thur 5pm–midnight; Fri–Sat 5pm–2am; $$
This cozy, den-like wine bar is a comfy place to rest your weary
feet and enjoy a glass of wine and a cheese plate after a busy
day walking and shopping around Union Square.

CIVIC CENTER AND HAYES VALLEY

The stunningly grand government and cultural buildings of San Francisco's Civic Center are sandwiched by the Tenderloin – one of the city's poorest areas – and the smart Hayes Valley, with its row of upscale boutiques, bars, galleries, and restaurants.

Compact Civic Center is awash with civic life and underpinned by city government, cultural institutions, and a cluster of visual and expressive arts venues. In the last 20 years, after redevelopment following the 1989 earth- quake, Hayes Valley has been transformed from an urban no-go area to one full of cutting-edge restauarants and some of the hippest shops in town.

SAN FRANCISCO PUBLIC LIBRARY, MAIN BRANCH

The imposing main branch of the Beaux Arts **San Francisco Public Library ❶** (100 Larkin Street; tel: 557-4400;

DISTANCE 1 mile (2km)
TIME 2–3 hours (this includes a visit to the Asian Art Museum)
START San Francisco Public Library
END Hayes and Laguna streets
POINTS TO NOTE
Because neighborhoods just outside the area covered by this tour can be unsafe, it is best not to wander off the path: the Tenderloin area to the north is as gritty as it gets. The tour begins at the San Francisco Public Library (BART: Civic Center station; bus: 5, 6, 7, 19, 21, 47, 49, 71 F).

Above: Hayes Valley design store; sculpture on the opera house.

Civic Art
Behind the public library's grand staircase is Nayland Blake's five-story *Constellation* (1996), an artwork that uses fiber-optic beams to illuminate inscriptions of 160 writers' names on glass shades. Blake's inspiration was a tradition begun by Paris's Bibliothèque Sainte-Geneviève: authors' names inscribed on its façade based on the location of their works inside.

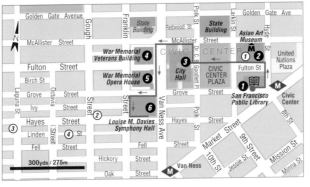

Beaux-Arts Style
In vogue from 1885–1920, this architectural movement combined Classical forms with Renaissance ideals, resulting in an eclectic neoclassical style. Symmetry, grandiose scale, and a profusion of architectural details number among its characteristics.

http://sfpl.lib.ca.us; Mon 10am–6pm, Tue–Thur 9am–8pm, Fri noon–6pm, Sat 10am–6pm, Sun noon–5pm) opened on April 18, 1996. Visitors are greeted by a stunning white granite façade, and inside, a lofty central atrium basks in natural light that pours in from a dramatic skylight. The third floor houses the American Center, the Chinese Center, and the James C. Hormel Gay & Lesbian Center. The last was the first resource center of its kind in a public institution, with books, photographs, films, and memorabilia documenting LGBT history and culture. Higher floors are home to music and environmental centers, which offer resources, information, and exhibits related to those subjects.

ASIAN ART MUSEUM

North of the library is the impressive **Asian Art Museum ②** (200 Larkin Street; tel: 581-3500; www.asianart.org; Tue–Sun 10am–5pm (Thur until 9pm); charge, 1st Sun of month free). In 2003, after decades in Golden Gate Park, the museum moved to this Beaux Arts building that had been redesigned by Gae Aulenti. The structure formerly hosted the main library; now instead of books, it has paintings, sculptures, ceramics, stoneware, basketry, puppets, weaponry, and textiles. With 17,000 artworks spanning 6,000 years of history, this is one of the world's most comprehensive collections of Asian art.

The Collection
Special rotating exhibits are shown on the first floor, while the second and third floors showcase around 2,500 pieces from the permanent collection in regionally grouped galleries that cover China, Japan, Korea, India, Iran, the Himalayas, and Southeast Asia.

Among the many highlights are Chinese jades and ceramics; Japanese bamboo baskets (the largest collection outside of Japan) and rare painted scrolls; Korean celadons and textiles; a Burmese 19th-century crowned and enthroned Buddha; Thai paintings; Indonesian puppets; Southeast Asian *krises* (daggers); Indian Buddhist stone sculptures; and Sikh art. One not-to-be-missed treasure is a gilded bronze Buddha on the third floor, inscribed A.D. 338; it is the oldest dated Chinese Buddha known in world. It is also one of some 7,700 objects donated by Avery Brundage, the Chicago industrialist whose endowment in the 1960s sparked the museum's creation.

Bimonthly tea-ceremony demonstrations (reservations recommended and extra charge required) are also held on site.

After or during your tour of the collections, you might wnat to stop off at the **Café Asia**, see ⑪①, to refuel.

Food and Drink 🍴

① CAFÉ ASIA
Asian Art Museum, 200 Larkin Street; tel: 581-3630; www.asianart.org/cafeasia.htm; Tue–Sun 10am-4:30pm (Thur to 8:30pm); $
Café Asia is a casual, convenient spot for refueling after touring the vast collections, with cafeteria-style service, indoor and outdoor seating, and plenty of Pan-Asian fare and café standards.

SAN FRANCISCO CITY HALL

Walk across the tree- and flag-lined walkways of Civic Center Plaza past lawns and sculptures to San Francisco's **City Hall** ❸ (1 Dr. Carlton B. Goodlett Place; tel: 554-4933; www.sfgov.org/site/cityhall; Mon–Fri 8am–8pm; free). Built in 1914 and occupying two spacious city blocks, the building was influenced by the City Beautiful movement of the 1890s and is perhaps the grandest seat of city government in the U.S., representing the city's optimism at the end of the century. The splendid 306ft (93m) bronze-and-gold-leaf dome that dominates the skyline is the fifth-largest in the world, dwarfing the U.S. Capitol Building in Washington D.C. by some 42in (107cm). San Fran-

cisco-based architect Arthur Brown, Jr. (1874–1957) designed the structure, including the finishing details such as doorknobs and floor patterns.

Inside, a wonderfully airy and open rotunda with white limestone walls and a floor of Tennessee pink marble serves as a backdrop for post-nuptial photo opportunities on the sweeping staircase. Back in 1954, City Hall witnessed the marriage of Joe DiMaggio and Marilyn Monroe. Flanking the rotunda are the North and South Light Courts; the latter is home to exhibits, artworks, and a clock with a design unique to City Hall, with the Roman numeral IV spelled (deliberately) as IIII.

City Hall was the scene of the murders of Harvey Milk and Mayor George

Historic Treaties

The War Memorial Opera House has also witnessed important diplomatic events. It was on the Opera House stage on June 26, 1945 that President Truman signed the United Nations charter, and the building also saw the signing of the San Francisco Peace Treaty between the United States and Japan, which officially ended hostilities between the two world powers in 1951.

Moscone in 1978, and in February 2004 it found itself at the center of nationwide controversy when Mayor Gavin Newsom granted marriage licenses to same-sex couples; around 4,000 flocked to City Hall to exchange their vows before the California Supreme Court shut down the proceedings. Sign up at the Docent Tour kiosk by the elevators in the Van Ness Avenue lobby for a 45-minute tour (tel: 554-6139; Mon–Fri 10am, noon and 2pm; free except for groups of eight or more).

WAR MEMORIAL VETERANS BUILDING

From City Hall walk north on Dr Carlton B. Goodlett Place and turn left on McAllister Street. Then turn left on Van Ness Avenue to reach the **War Memorial Veterans Building** ❹ at

No. 401, one of a pair of nearly identical Beaux Arts buildings that comprise the War Memorial Complex. The Veterans Building is home to the 916-seat **Herbst Theater** as well as the **San Francisco Arts Commission Gallery** (tel: 554-6080; www.sfacgallery.org; Wed–Sat noon–5pm; free), with its diverse contemporary art exhibits.

WAR MEMORIAL OPERA HOUSE

Continue walking south on Van Ness Avenue, reaching the **War Memorial Opera House** ❺ at No. 301. The building features a long, marble-floored foyer, a vaulted and coffered ceiling, and a handsome 3,146-seat hall, through which the first aria soared on October 15, 1932, to the tune of Giacomo Puccini's *Tosca*.

Food and Drink

② ARLEQUIN TO GO

384 Hayes Street; tel: 626-1211; Mon–Fri 8am–7pm, Sat 9am–7pm, Sun 9am–6pm; $

Do not let the name fool you: this small café opens up to a wide, lush garden in the back, and is a great place to enjoy top-quality café food with an espresso or a glass of beer or wine.

③ SUPPENKÜCHE

525 Laguna Street; tel: 252-9289; www.suppenkuche.com; Mon–Sat D only, Sun Br and D; $$

One of the few German restaurants in the city, where huge portions of updated German classics – *spaetzle*, schnitzel, potato pancakes, and wonderful, hearty soups – are served in a convivial atmosphere to diners who sit family-style on long spartan benches. Around 20 beers (mostly German) are on tap.

④ BLUE BOTTLE COFFEE COMPANY

315 Linden Street; www.bluebottlecoffee.net; Mon–Fri 7am–5pm, Sat–Sun 8am–5pm; $

This tiny to-go kiosk serves espressos, drip coffee, New Orleans iced coffee, cookies and *biscotti*. It may be small, but its quality coffee brings it a lot of business.

The **San Francisco Opera** (tel: 861-4008, box office 864-3330; www.sfopera.com) performs here September–November and May–July. During its off-season, the **San Francisco Ballet** (tel: 865-2000; www.sfballet.org) takes the stage, presenting traditional ballets and modern dance, and a very popular *Nutcracker* production each December.

LOUISE M. DAVIES SYMPHONY HALL

Just across Grove Street, the elegant **Louise M. Davies Symphony Hall ❻** (201 Van Ness Avenue) houses the **San Francisco Symphony Orchestra** (tel: 552-8000; www.sfsymphony.org), whose main season runs September–July. From Van Ness, turn right on Grove Street, left on Franklin Street, and right on Hayes Street.

HAYES VALLEY

After the 1989 earthquake rendered unsafe a portion of the Central Freeway that hovered menacingly over Hayes Valley, a large chunk of it was removed and the once drug- and prostitute-riddled neighborhood shifted suddenly into a hip retail center with flashy fashions, art galleries, specialty stores, and a melting pot of international cuisines at cheery restaurants and low-key bars.

To soak up the Hayes Valley shopping scene, walk west on Hayes Street to Laguna Street. You might like to stop for a bite at **Arlequin To Go**, see ⑪②, or walk a few blocks more for hearty Bavarian cuisine at **Suppenküche**, see ⑪③. If caffeine is all you crave, turn left onto Octavia Street and then left onto Linden Street, for the **Blue Bottle Coffee Company**, see ⑪④.

Hayes Boutiques

Hayes Street squeezes in a terrific collection of boutiques between Franklin and Laguna Streets. Nancy Boy (347 Hayes Street; tel: 552-3802; www.nancyboy.com; Mon–Fri 11am–7pm, Sat–Sun 11am–6pm) markets upscale men's body products with the playful slogan, "Tested on Boyfriends – Not Animals." Flight 001 (525 Hayes Street; tel: 487-1001; www.flight001.com; Mon–Sat 11am–7pm, Sun 11am–6pm) supplies mod jet-setting gear in zesty colors, from sleek luggage to silk eye-masks. Alternatively, Alabaster (597 Hayes Street; tel: 558-0482; www.alabastersf.com; Tue–Sat 11am–6pm, Sun noon–5pm) offers creamy alabaster lamps and an eclectic assortment of other elegant home ornaments. These blocks also pack in several excellent new and vintage-clothing boutiques.

NOB HILL AND RUSSIAN HILL

Soak up Nob Hill's old-fashioned refinement with its grand hotels and the Gothic Grace Cathedral and then explore tony Russian Hill's hidden stairways, crooked streets, and charming cafés, restaurants, and boutiques.

What's in a Name?
Some believe the word "Nob" was derived from "nabob," a British term for the rich that was derived from the Indian word for Moghul prince; others say Nob is simply a version of "knob," meaning a rounded hill. Many San Franciscans like to use yet another moniker, "Snob Hill."

DISTANCE 2½ miles (4km)
TIME A half-day
START Inter-Continental Mark Hopkins San Francisco
END Polk Street
POINTS TO NOTE
This tour's several very steep hills and stairways make it unsuitable for wheelchair-users. To reach the starting point: bus: 1 to Mason Street; cable-car: Powell–Hyde or Powell–Mason line to California Street, or California line to Mason Street

Nob Hill Spa
The Nob Hill Spa may be the most luxurious day spa, but the city has an entire menu of healing and beauty arts on tap, from walk-in yoga classes to nail salons. One of the most exotic spas is lavender-scented Kabuki Springs in Japantown, with candlelit baths perfect for tired tourists. Tel: 415-922-6000.

This tour begins on the crest of stately Nob Hill, at California and Mason streets. With its imposing hotels and breathtaking vistas, Nob Hill exudes grandeur and good breeding, offering a glimpse of the pomp and decadence of the early days of San Francisco. Formerly known as California Hill, Nob Hill was originally just steeply sloped scrubland. With the advent of the cable-car, however, its peak became easily accessible and allowed the city's elite to turn it into an exclusive neighborhood of fine mansions and restaurants some 376ft (115m) above the existing city.

EXCLUSIVE ENCLAVE

Nicknamed the "hill of palaces" by the Scottish writer Robert Louis Stevenson, Nob Hill has always had a reputation for being home to privilege and luxury, and was where the "Big Four" of the Central Pacific Railroad – Leland Stanford, Charles Crocker, Mark Hopkins, and Collis Huntington – built opulent estates, only to see them demolished by the 1906 earthquake and fire. From the ashes of their mansions rose world-famous luxury hotels, continuing the neighborhood's tradition of privilege. The stratospheric rates keep these hotels exclusive, but all are welcome to view their lobbies or buy a drink at the bar.

Inter-Continental Mark Hopkins
The southeast corner of California and Mason streets hosts the towering **Inter-Continental Mark Hopkins San Francisco ❶** (1 Nob Hill; tel: 392-3434; www.markhopkins.net), opened to great fanfare in 1926 on the former site of railway tycoon Mark Hopkins's mansion. The hotel bespeaks sky-high class, all the way up to the 19th-floor **Top of the Mark** bar and its tall crow's nest, where the largest U.S. flag flying in San Francisco proudly flaps.

Renaissance Stanford Court

Look east to 905 California for the **Renaissance Stanford Court Hotel** ❷ (tel: 989-3500; www.marriott.com/hotels/travel/sfosc-the-stanford-court-a-renaissance-hotel). Another result of the 1906 destruction, this hotel was built in 1911 in the place of the ruined mansion of Leland Stanford, who lent his name to the university he founded with his wife in Palo Alto, California.

The Fairmont San Francisco

Walk north on Mason Street past the regal-looking **Fairmont San Francisco** ❸ (950 Mason Street; tel: 772-5000; www.fairmont.com/san francisco), a hotel that once dominated the San Francisco skyline, and where Tony Bennett first sang *I Left My Heart in San Francisco*.

Built by Tessie and Virginia Fair as a lavish testament to their father James "Bonanza Jim" Graham Fair (once one of the richest men in San Francisco), the hotel was completed just before the 1906 disaster only to have the sumptuous interiors ruined by the fire. It was speedily rebuilt, with the remodeling overseen by Julia Morgan, and re-opened triumphantly just a year to the day after the devastating event.

PACIFIC-UNION CLUB

Now the private, prestigious, and men-only **Pacific-Union Club** ❹, the brownstone across Mason Street from the Fairmont was the only neighborhood estate left standing after the 1906 disaster. Built by silver magnate James Cair Flood, the Connecticut sandstone building, designed by Willis Polk, is considered the first of its kind to be constructed west of the Mississippi.

BROCKLEBANK BUILDING

Walk north on Mason to the corner of Mason and Sacramento streets to enjoy fine vistas to the north and east.

Above from far left: there are great views from Nob and Russian hills down toward the sea; stained-glass interior dome of the Fairmont San Francisco; Nob Hill Spa; exterior of the Fairmont.

Above from left:
holiday snapping;
glitzy Gates of
Paradise at Grace
Cathedral; stained-
glass windows at
Grace Cathedral.

This brings you to the **Brocklebank Building** ❺, former home of legendary *San Francisco Chronicle* columnist Herb Caen. The building may look familiar to enthusiasts of film director Alfred Hitchcock: along with a flashy forest-green Jaguar parked out front, it featured in his San Francisco-set film classic, *Vertigo* (1958).

HUNTINGTON PARK

Walk west on Sacramento to reach the genteel greenery of bench-lined **Huntington Park** ❻. Once the site of railroad lawyer David Colton's mansion, this is a lovely place to lounge, browse an occasional weekend art show, enjoy the view of neighboring Grace Cathedral, and do some people-watching. The central fountain is a replica of the Tartarughe Fountain in Rome's Piazza Mattei.

GRACE CATHEDRAL

Across Taylor Street from Huntington Park, climb the cascade of white steps to stately **Grace Cathedral** ❼ (1100 California Street; tel: 749-6300; www. gracecathedral.org; Sun–Fri 7am–6pm, Sat 8am–6pm; donation appreciated), which sits on land gifted by the Charles Crocker family.

Finished in 1964, the cathedral is an Episcopal tribute to the French Gothic style. Outside the east entrance are casts of Lorenzo Ghiberti's 15th-century, 16-ft (5-m) high, bronze-and-gold doors, called the **Gates of Paradise**. Originally sculpted for the Baptistery of the cathedral in Florence, they depict stories from the Old and New testaments.

The Interior

Inside the cathedral, colorful paintings decorate the walls, and light streams

Cable-Car Central

San Francisco's Cable-Car Museum is the nerve center of the transportation system invented by London-born American immigrant Andrew Smith Hallidie (1836–1900), that was once ridiculed as "Hallidie's Folly," because no one thought it would actually work. Here, electric motors drive the huge winding machinery, which keep the cables running through slots in the street at a constant speed of 9½mph (15kph). Today there are 40 cable-cars in the city's system, with a maximum of 26 running along the three lines at any given time. It may seem impressive that a cable-car can take you all the way from Market and Powell streets to Fisherman's Wharf, but the 4¾ miles (8km) of track in use is nothing compared to the 75 miles (121km) along which the eight original companies' cable-cars used to creak.

through stained glass of rich blues, reds, and yellows. Charles Connick's **23rd Psalm Window** above the southern entrance echoes Chartres Cathedral's Jesse Window, while Gabriel Loire's **Rose Window** above the east entrance depicts St. Francis's poem *The Canticle of the Sun*. A small recess houses the **Aids Interfaith Chapel**, which is dedicated to those affected by Aids. The chapel features an altarpiece by Keith Haring as well as a colorful panel from the Aids Memorial Quilt (www.aids quilt.org), a project begun in 1987 when the devastating epidemic was ravaging San Francisco. The cathedral also features two **labyrinths** that are used for traditional meditative walking.

CABLE-CAR MUSEUM

Exit the church and turn left onto the quietly picturesque Taylor Street. If you are hungry, nab a sidewalk table at **Nob Hill Café**, see ⑪①. Keep your eyes peeled for matchy-matchy Marian and Vivian Brown, the famous octogenarian "San Francisco twins," known for their signature identical outfits who live in the neighborhood, Turn right at Washington and teeter down towards the red brick **Cable-Car Museum ❽** (1201 Mason Street; tel: 474-1887; www. cablecarmuseum.org; daily 10am–5pm, Apr–Sept to 6pm; free). Built in 1910, this historic cable-car barn and powerhouse displays antique cable-cars, engines, winding wheels, and other mechanical devices that help the beloved moving National Monuments run smoothly.

INA COOLBRITH PARK

Walk north on Mason Street. At Vallejo Street turn left to reach the stairways marking the entrance of the **Ina Coolbrith Park ❾**. Coolbrith was an Oakland librarian and California's first poet laureate; she also mentored a young Jack London and entertained other literary greats at her home on nearby Macondray Lane *(see next page)*. These steep stairways climb to small, narrow lookout ledges peppered with pine trees, cacti, and green benches. Though a challenging climb, it offers dramatic, sweeping panoramas of North Beach, Telegraph Hill, and Coit Tower, the length of Bay Bridge, the TransAmerica building, and downtown San Francisco. Now you have reached the breezy top of upscale Russian Hill, named for the Russians buried in a cemetery here in the early days of San Francisco.

FEUSIER HOUSE AND 1907 FIREHOUSE

When you emerge from the park you will be on Vallejo Street; walk down to Jones Street and turn right. Then turn left at Green Street to reach the **Feusier House ❿**, an eight-sided oddity built in 1857 when octagonal

Above: Grace Cathedral; Nob Hill mansion.

Food and Drink

① NOB HILL CAFÉ

1152 Taylor Street; tel: 776-6500; daily L and D; $$

This cozy neighborhood bistro features delicious northern Italian cuisine and is loved by locals for its great wine, ambience and the ethereal tiramisu. They do not take reservations, so be sure to get there early, or be prepared to wait in line.

Above from left:
Oyster restaurant on
Polk Street; Nob Hill
at sunset.

houses were thought to be economical and healthy due to increased sunlight and better ventilation. Across the street at 1088 Green Street is the old **1907 Firehouse ⓫**, bought from the city in 1957 by Louise M. Davies, for whom the city's symphony hall is named. Both houses are private residences and closed to the public. Return to Jones Street and turn left, descending the steps on the east side. On Jones between Green and Union

streets, sneak a peek down **Macondray Lane ⓬**, a beautifully woodsy and secluded lane with a secret-garden ambience. Turn left at Chestnut Street.

SAN FRANCISCO ART INSTITUTE

At 800 Chestnut Street stands the **San Francisco Art Institute ⓭** (tel: 771-7020; www.sfai.edu; Tue–Sat 11am–6pm; free), an educational establish-

Right: snaking
Lombard Street.

ment founded in 1871, which also hosts temporary exhibits open to the public. Pass through the courtyard to the gallery on the left, which houses the institute's most important permanent work of art, *Making of a Fresco Showing the Building of a City* (1931) by Mexican artist Diego Rivera. The fresco within a fresco features Rivera on a scaffold surrounded by others who worked on the artwork. Step onto the fresh breeze-swept concrete terraces to enjoy a bite at the café, see ⑴②, and to soak up views of the bay, North Beach, Coit Tower, and Russian Hill.

LOMBARD STREET

Continue up Chestnut Street and turn left at Leavenworth Street. Pass the twin gazebos and rose bushes of dime-sized **Fay Park** ⑭ on the left (Wed–Thur and Sun 10am–4pm). This historic Thomas Church garden was designed in 1957 and bequeathed to the city in 1998. Turn right up the famously twisty **Lombard Street** ⑮, a one-way block with eight hairpin turns. Although known as the "crookedest street in the world," San Francisco's own Vermont Avenue at 20th Street is actually more bendy. Climb Lombard, admiring the flowery landscaping and ivy-covered private residences.

HYDE AND POLK STREETS

Turn left onto leafy Hyde Street, lined with clusters of cafés, elegant bistros, and antique stores, and traversed by the whirring Powell–Hyde cable-car. As

you pass Filbert Street, note the sudden drop-off on the left after half a block; the 31.5 percent gradient descent is the city's steepest. At Hyde and Union, order an ice cream at **Swensen's**, see ⑴③, a city institution. End the tour with dinner at Hyde Street's **Sushi Groove**, see ⑴④, or turn right on Green Street and dine in the Russian Hill hub of **Polk Street**, see ⑴⑤ and ⑴⑥, a mishmash of trendy cafés, boutiques, restaurants, and night spots.

Literary Connection
Overgrown and lined with paths of uneven brick and stone, it is the real-life counterpart to Barbary Lane in Armistead Maupin's *Tales of the City*, a series that chronicled life in San Francisco from the mid-1970s to the mid-1980s.

Food and Drink

② SAN FRANCISCO ART INSTITUTE CAFÉ
800 Chestnut Street; tel: 749-4567; fall–spring: Mon–Thur 9am–5pm, Fri 9am–4pm, summer: 9am–2pm; $
Perched on top of the school, this casual café has spectacular views of the Golden Gate, Alcatraz, Angel Island and the East Bay, and is the place to be on a hot day.

③ SWENSEN'S
1999 Hyde Street; tel: 775-6818; Tue–Sun noon–10pm; $
Earle Swensen opened his first Ice Cream Shoppe here in 1948, whipping up ice cream as "Good as Father Used to Make." Fifty years later, Swensen's is still dishing up flavorful scoops that will have you licking your lips for more.

④ SUSHI GROOVE
1916 Hyde Street; tel: 440-1905; daily D; $$
A young and sophisticated crowd cozies up in this intimate but lively spot, where fresh sushi and varied sake are served against a backdrop of modern decor and acid jazz and chill techno tunes.

⑤ YABBIE'S COASTAL KITCHEN
2237 Polk Street; tel: 474-4088; www.yabbiesrestaurant.com; daily D; $$$
An oyster bar, wine bar, and dining rooms where delicious seafood is offered with friendly service in a relaxed but classy setting.

⑥ NICK'S CRISPY TACOS
1500 Broadway Street; tel: 409-8226; daily L and D; $
Locals rave about the cheap, delicious tacos at this ultra-relaxed joint. No one wastes time with the burritos, just order your tacos "Nick's Way" and you will not be disappointed.

8 JAPANTOWN, PACIFIC HEIGHTS, AND COW HOLLOW

Wander from Japantown through affluent Pacific Heights and its neighbor Cow Hollow, soaking up the handsome architecture of private mansions and townhouses, lovely hilltop parks with dramatic views, and chic cafés, restaurants, and boutiques.

Swanky Spas

The Pacific Heights area is home to several of San Francisco's plush pampering options. In Japantown, Kabuki Springs and Spa (1750 Geary Boulevard; tel: 922-6000; www.kabuki springs.com; daily 10am–9:45pm) is a serene setting for facials, acupuncture, massages, and traditional communal baths. Named for the eye-popping paint hue used on the Golden Gate Bridge, International Orange (2nd floor, 2044 Fillmore Street; tel: 888-894-8811; www. internationalorange. com; Mon–Fri 9am–9pm, Sat–Sun 9am–8pm) is a fresh-feeling day spa with a relaxing redwood sundeck. It offers yoga classes and treatments, including massage therapies.

DISTANCE 3 miles (5km)
TIME A half-day
START Japan Center
END Union and Gough streets
POINTS TO NOTE
The Haas-Lilienthal House tour is only offered Wed, Sat, or Sun afternoons. Unless otherwise noted, the residences mentioned are closed to the public, and the privacy of the owners should be respected.
This tour begins at the Japan Center (bus: 1, 3, 12, 22, 24).

Largely residential, the three central neighborhoods of Japantown, Pacific Heights, and Cow Hollow all have their own thriving commercial centers and boast some of the best examples of San Francisco architecture. Fillmore Street is a major north–south route that links the three.

JAPANTOWN

Compact Japantown is home to the city's 12,000 resident Japanese commu-

nity and is dominated by the **Japan Center ❶** (Post Street, between Fillmore and Laguna streets; www.sfjapan town.org). This 5-acre (2-hectare) complex of Japanese restaurants and boutiques designed by Minoru Yamasaki is filled with elegant home decor, vintage silk kimonos, and Japanese-language books. The **Peace Plaza** is home to the Peace Pagoda designed by Yoshiro Taniguchi and presented in friendship to the people of the U.S. from the people of Japan after World War II.

Exit onto Post Street and turn left, passing the **Sundance Kabuki ❷** (1881 Post Street; tel: 929-4650; www.sun dancecinemas.com/kabuki.html). This upscale, remodeled theater presents independent films and blockbusters, as well as much of the San Francisco International Film Festival, held every spring.

FILLMORE STREET

Continue along Post Street and turn right at Fillmore Street, *the* place to enjoy the luxury of Pacific Heights. Pick up some French pastries at **La Boulange**, see ⑪①, or a cup of rich

hot chocolate farther along at **Bitter-sweet**, see ①②, then walk north, browsing the glossy boutiques. For a more substantial start on weekends, try brunch at **Elite Café**, see ①③. Continue north to find the **Clay Theatre** ③ (2261 Fillmore Street; tel: 267-4893; www.landmarktheatres.com). Of the dying, single-screen breed, this comfy one-time nickelodeon built in 1910 now hosts independent films and popular midnight screenings.

ALTA PLAZA PARK

From Fillmore Street, detour left on Washington Street to reach **Alta Plaza Park** ④, designed by the legendary Golden Gate Park landscaper John McLaren. Staggered stairways climb grassy terraces to reach basketball and tennis courts, and sweeping city views.

LAFAYETTE PARK

For even more views, backtrack along Washington Street to cross Fillmore Street and continue on to **Lafayette Park** ⑤. Here, you can take in the beautiful panoramas from a four-block swathe of greenery that is dusted with pinecones and eucalyptus leaves, and surrounded by stately Pacific Heights mansions.

SPRECKELS MANSION

On the north side of Lafayette Park, sneak a peek north at the grand Beaux-Arts **Spreckels Mansion** ⑥ (2080 Washington Street), partially obscured by tall shrubbery. Built in 1913 for Alma de Bretteville Spreckels and her sugar-heir husband Adolph Spreckels (the same Spreck that

Above from far left: stylish sushi; Japanese doll; detail of a local plaque; the Peace Plaza.

Above: Buddha statue in a local spa; Japanese paper shop.

Food and Drink 🍴

① LA BOULANGE AT FILLMORE
2043 Fillmore Street; tel: 928-1300; www.baybread.com; daily 7am–6pm; $
Just around the corner from the original, "mother" bakery, La Boulangerie (2325 Pine Street), this spot delights with flaky French pastries, organic coffee and espresso, open-faced sandwiches, and old-fashioned burgers.

② BITTERSWEET
2123 Fillmore Street; tel: 346-8715; www.bittersweetcafe.com; daily 10am–8pm (Fri–Sat until 10pm); $
Indulge in rich and decadent drinks, from a cup of creamy and classic hot chocolate to a cardamom-infused, Venezuelan white chocolate concoction. Also offered are hand-rolled ganache truffles, scones, muffins and other baked goods, and 120 different kinds of chocolate bar from around the world.

③ ELITE CAFÉ
2049 Fillmore Street; tel: 346-8668; Mon–Fri D only, Sat–Sun Br and D; $$
This tried-and-true locals' fave serves Cajun- and Creole-inspired seafood dishes in a cheery atmosphere. An excellent raw bar beckons, as does the Cajun brunch, with perfectly seasoned Bloody Marys.

Shopping Tips
Among Fillmore Street's stylish offerings are international fashion-forward footwear at Gimme Shoes (No. 2358; tel: 441-3040; www.gimmeshoes. com; Mon–Sat 11am–7pm, Sun 11am–6pm) and whimsical, Parisian-style home goods at Nest (No. 2300; tel: 292-6199; www.nestsf.com; Mon–Fri 10:30am–6:30pm, Sat 10:30am–6pm, Sun 11am–6pm).

Above: Pacific Heights' mansions *(top and bottom)* and flag for the local Jazz Festival *(middle)*.

Haunted House
Over the years, people have reported ghostly sightings or a ghostly presence in the basement of the Whittier Mansion. Most believe it is the ghost of Whittier himself, who died in 1917, but others suggest it is his ne'er-do-well son Billy, who when alive, used to frequent the servants' quarters and his father's wine cellar for "wine, women, and song."

donated the Palace of the Legion of Honor Art Museum to the City of San Francisco in 1924), the imposing white limestone contains 55 rooms, including a Louis XVI-style ball-room. Now the residence is owned by the romantic novelist Danielle Steele.

HAAS-LILIENTHAL HOUSE

Continue east on Washington Street and turn north on Franklin Street to

tour the **Haas-Lilienthal House** ❼ (No. 2007; tel: 441-3004; www.sf heritage.org/house.html; tours Wed and Sat noon–3pm, Sun 11am–4pm; call in advance on Sat as is sometimes closed for private functions; charge). This Queen Anne-style Victorian mansion with elaborate wooden gables was designed by Bavarian architect Peter Schmidt and built in 1886. It is the city's only intact Victorian from the period to be regularly open as a

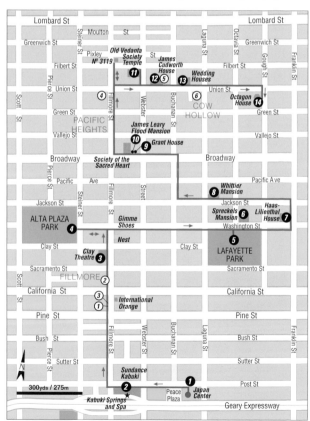

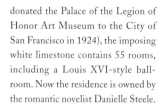

museum, complete with original furniture and artifacts, and was occupied by the same family until 1972.

WHITTIER MANSION

Continuing on Franklin, turn left onto Jackson Street to reach the **Whittier Mansion ❸** (No. 2090), built in 1896 for William Frank Whittier, a prominent businessman. Designed by Edward R. Swain, the building survived the 1906 earthquake thanks to its construction of stone on a steel framework, then a state-of-the-art technique in San Francisco.

JAMES LEARY FLOOD MANSION

At this point in the tour, continue on Franklin and turn right on Buchanan Street and left on Broadway Street to reach the school quarters and administrative buildings of the **Society of the Sacred Heart**. The **Grant House ❾** (No. 2220) and its exquisite neighbor, the three-story **James Leary Flood Mansion ❿** (No. 2222; tel: 563-2900; www.floodmansion.org) form part of the complex.

Designed in 1912 by Bliss and Faville and completed in time for the 1915 Panama-Pacific World Exposition, the former Flood residence is a stunning combination of architecture styles. A courtyard on the north side of the house offers a dazzling view of the bay, while the interiors are beautifully dressed in marble, hand-carved woods, and hand-painted murals.

3119 FILLMORE STREET

From Broadway, turn right on Fillmore Street for a steep descent to Union Street. On October 13, 1955, Allen Ginsberg first performed his legendary poem *Howl*, at the now-defunct Gallery Six that used to occupy 3119 Fillmore Street. Ginsberg ended the reading in tears, the audience went wild, and Jack Kerouac declared, "Ginsberg, this poem will make you famous in San Francisco."

Above from far left: panoramic views from Alta Plaza Park *(see p.65)*; hilly Pacific Heights.

Below: the Haas-Lilienthal House.

Beat Buddies
The Beats put the city's literary scene on the map, and Allen Ginsberg was one of the key players. His friend and fellow Beatnik Jack Kerouac memorialized the epic night of October 13, 1955, when one of the characters in his 1958 novel *Dharma Bums* recited the poem *Wail*.

OLD VEDANTA SOCIETY TEMPLE

Turn left on Union Street for French bistro fare at **Chez Maman**, see ⑪④, otherwise turn right on Union Street and left on Webster Street to reach the turreted, lavender-hued **Old Vedanta Society Temple** ⑪ (No. 2963; www.sfvedanta.org), built in 1906. In line with its mission "to promote harmony between Eastern and Western thought, and recognition of the truth in all the great religions of the world," each of the temple's unique towers represents a different major world religious tradition. It is thought to be the first Hindu temple built in the West.

UNION STREET

From the temple, return to Union Street and turn left into the heart of yuppie Cow Hollow, named for the cow pastures and dairy-farming industry that once dominated the area. At No. 2040, the old farmhouse of dairy rancher James Cudworth ⑫ stands as evidence from that era.

Nearby at No. 1980 are the wedding presents Cudworth built for his daughters: a pair of identical Victorians known as the **Wedding Houses** ⑬ that share a front porch. Today, Cow Hollow brims with the cream of the crop, filled with fine boutiques, trendy eateries, corner cafés, and singles-scene bars that are all frequented by preppy young professionals.

Stop for nourishment either at Pan-Asian **Betelnut**, see ⑪⑤ or the **Bus Stop** sports bar, see ⑪⑥, or at one of the many other eateries clustered along Union Street.

OCTAGON HOUSE

Turn right on Gough Street and end the tour at the quaint, eight-sided building, the **Octagon House** ⑭ (No. 2645; tel: 441-7512; Feb–Dec 2nd Sun of month, 2nd and 4th Thur of month noon–3pm; donation appreciated).

Food and Drink 🍴

④ CHEZ MAMAN
2223 Union Street; tel: 771-7771; www.chezmamansf; Mon–Sat L and D; $$
A French bistro without attitude, Chez Maman has in a few short years become a casual favorite for Cow Hollow locals, who love the simple, tasty, and inexpensive cuisine. The endearing house rule is that you must finish your plate – not that this should be a hardship.

⑤ BETELNUT
2030 Union Street; tel: 929-8855; www.betelnutrestaurant.com; Tue–Sun L and D; $$
A Pan-Asian bar-restaurant specializing in dumplings and noodle bowls with bold, exciting flavors.

⑥ BUS STOP
1901 Union Street; tel: 567-6905; www.busstopbar.com; Mon–Fri 10am–2am, Sat–Sun 9am–2am; $
In the heart of Cow Hollow, this sports bar quickly fills up with twenty- and thirtysomethings drinking well-poured drinks and affordable beer while watching sports and each other.

Popular in the mid-19th century, eight-sided houses *(see also the Feusier House, p.61)* were advocated for their health benefits, namely increased sunlight and better ventilation afforded by the cupola. Built in 1861 by William C. McElroy and now a San Francisco Historical Landmark, the cottage-like structure looks like it has popped out of a fairy tale; it is painted a pale blue, frosted with white trimming, and framed by a picket fence. Inside are items of period furniture, documents, and decorative arts.

Above from far left: Old Vedanta Society Temple; boutique in Pacific Heights; row of Victorian houses in Japantown *(see p.64).*

Left: steep streets in Pacific Heights.

GOLDEN GATE PARK AND HAIGHT-ASHBURY

The sprawling Golden Gate Park is perfect for whiling away time out of doors, filled with fields, gardens, and lakes and home to the de Young Museum. Equally laid-back is the scruffier Haight Street, a counterculture landmark cluttered with thrift shops and cheap eateries.

Above: the de Young Museum; safety-pin artwork outside the de Young Museum; five-story Japanese pagoda in Golden Gate Park.

DISTANCE 3 miles (5km)

TIME A full day

START de Young Museum

END Haight-Ashbury

POINTS TO NOTE

Although Golden Gate Park is immense, do not worry too much about getting lost in the wilderness. Paths are well marked, with signs and maps pointing you in the direction of various major attractions. This tour begins at the de Young Museum. The 5 and 21 buses stop at 8th and Fulton streets, just outside the park. Walk into the park and turn right on John F. Kennedy Drive to reach the museum's tower entrance. To return downtown from the Haight, take the 7 or 71 buses that run along the full length of Haight Street, or the 6, which makes its first stop on Haight at Masonic.

One of San Francisco's icons, Golden Gate Park represents the late-19th-century aspirations of civic leaders who sought to build a city (and a park) rivaling New York. Haight-Ashbury, on the other hand, came to represent the aspirations of the hippie movement, whose roots lay in the countercultural values of the Beat Generation.

GOLDEN GATE PARK

Where rolling sand dunes could once be seen, Golden Gate Park's grassy hills now carpet over 1,000 acres (405 hectares) of land that stretches 52 blocks from the edge of the Haight-Ashbury neighborhood to the Pacific Ocean. Surrounded by gardens and groves, it is easy to forget about the hustle and bustle of the city, especially on Sundays, when John F. Kennedy Drive is closed to car traffic. Sporty people converge on the park to take advantage of fields and miles of trails to run and bike along, not to mention the golf course, polo and archery fields, tennis courts, and fly-fishing pond. Others picnic, barbeque, and nap on the lawns. The San Francisco Parks Trust offers free walking tours; call the 24-hour hotline (263-0991) for times.

De Young Museum

In 2005, the **de Young Museum ❶** (50 Hagiwara Tea Garden Drive; tel: 750-3600; www.famsf.org/deyoung;

Tue–Sun 9:30am–5:15pm (Fri until 8:45pm); charge, 1st Tue of month free) reopened in Golden Gate Park in a bold facility that replaced the one severely damaged by the 1989 Loma Prieta earthquake. The controversial design features a copper-clad exterior that will oxidize over time and a nine-story observation tower that sticks out (literally and figuratively) in the natural park setting *(see margin tip).*

Several fine collections are displayed in the spacious, light-filled interior: the concourse level hosts 20th-century and contemporary art (including works by Georgia O'Keeffe, Edward Hopper, and Grant Wood), art from the Americas, Native American art, and a room of murals, while upstairs are rare works from Africa, Oceania, and New Guinea, plus early American artworks and separate textile and photography exhibits.

The museum also has a sculpture garden, museum store, and café, and mounts immensely popular special exhibitions, featuring works from the likes of photographer Annie Leibovitz and glass artist Dale Chihuly.

Japanese Tea Garden

Just west of the de Young along Hagiwara Tea Garden Drive is the **Japanese Tea Garden ❷** (tel: 752-1171; www.sfpt.org; daily 9am–6pm; charge). This peaceful setting of cherry blossoms, bonsai conifers, carp ponds, and wooden bridges is the oldest public Japanese-style garden in the country, and a popular place to wander and snack on tea and cookies sold in the garden's teahouse.

California Academy of Sciences

Cross the 20,000-seat **Music Concourse ❸** – an outdoor summer music venue completed in 1900 and landscaped with fountains and trees – to reach the **California Academy of Sciences ❹** (55 Music Concourse Drive; tel: 379-8000; www.calacademy.org; Mon–Sat 9:30am–5pm, Sun 11am–5pm; charge, 3rd Wed of month free). The academy reopened in Golden Gate Park after much anticipation. Italian-born Pritzker Prize-winning architect Renzo Piano designed the structure, which integrates the archi-

Above from far left: sunbathing in Golden Gate Park; prime specimen in the Dahlia Garden; chilling in a café in bohemian Haight-Ashbury; the lake in Golden Gate Park.

View from Above
From the top of the de Young's twisting 144ft (44m) copper observation tower, the amazing panorama of San Francisco's cityscape is as stunning a work of art as any you might find inside the museum. On a clear day, the 360-degree floor-to-ceiling windows reveal the city in all its glory.

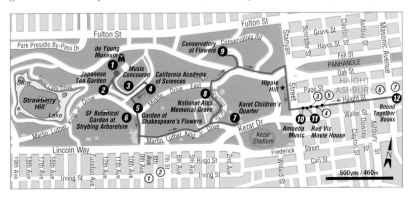

Stow Lake

Head over to Stow Lake, in the western part of the park, to rent rowboats and paddle boats (tel: 752-0347; charge) and spend a leisurely afternoon gliding around with the turtles). This is the largest of the park's 11 lakes, and Strawberry Hill, at its center, provides the park's highest vantage point.

tecture with the park's natural setting through sustainable features such as a living roof, solar panels, and water reclamation. The interactive natural history museum boasts a collection of some 18 million scientific specimens, including plants, animals, fossils, and artifacts. The Steinhart Aquarium is home to a bright array of exotic fish and other swimming and slithering species. Also on site are a live coral reef and a large natural history collection from the Galapagos Islands.

Garden of Shakespeare's Flowers

Exit the Academy on Music Concourse Drive and turn left on Martin Luther King Jr. Drive. Turn left again into the **Garden of Shakespeare's Flowers ❺**, a collection of flowers and herbs that are mentioned in poems and plays penned by the bard, accompanied by plaques engraved with relevant quotations.

San Francisco Botanical Garden

Continue south on Martin Luther King Jr. Drive to reach the **San Fran-**

Right: Conservatory of Flowers (see p.74).

cisco **Botanical Garden at Strybing Arboretum ❻** (9th Avenue and Lincoln Way; tel: 661-1316; www.sf botanicalgarden.org; Mon–Fri 8am–4:30pm, Sat–Sun 10am–5pm; free). From Mediterranean to tropical cloud-forest plants, the 7,500 diverse species found here come from all around the globe. A "Garden of Fragrance" is one of several specialty gardens, and free guided walks are offered daily at 1:30pm. Alternatively, join the multitudes that choose the grass outside the Arboretum in which to relax and soak up the sun.

Koret Children's Quarter
Walk east on Martin Luther King Jr. for about a mile. If you are hungry, turn right on 7th Avenue for lunch options in the Inner Sunset neighborhood. Choose from seafood, see ⑪①, Indian cuisine, see ⑪②, or one of the many other eateries on Irving Street. Return to Martin Luther King Jr. Drive, pass the baseball diamonds on your left, and enter the historic **Koret Children's Quarter ❼**.

Formerly known as the Children's Playground, this public playground built in 1887 is oldest in the U.S. Nearby, youngsters ride on the colorful carrousel (charge), which was carved in 1912 and was one of the main carrousels at the 1939 World's Fair on San Francisco's Treasure Island. Look north and you will see **Hippie Hill**, home to ad hoc musical celebrations on weekends, with dozens of locals letting loose with drums, shakers, or whatever else they can find, from pans

to sticks. Hula-hoops and roller skates are optional.

National Aids Memorial Grove
Walk west to and head north along Bowling Green Drive; at its intersection with Middle Drive East is the main portal of the **National Aids Memorial Grove ❽** (tel: 765-0497; www.aids memorial.org; free). Over seven wooded acres (3 hectares) comprise this peaceful, living tribute to those whose lives have been affected either directly or indirectly

Above from far left: the Garden of Shakespeare's Flowers; fun in the Koret Children's Quarter; the park's stark and moving tribute to Aids victims and their loved ones; afternoon snooze in the National Aids Memorial Grove.

Food and Drink 🍴

① PJ'S OYSTER BED
737 Irving Street; tel: 566-7775; daily L and D; $$
An open kitchen and Mardi Gras nights keep this delicious and fun seafood restaurant in the heart of the Inner Sunset neighborhood hopping. No gimmicks here, just fresh and flavorful food.

② NAAN 'N' CURRY
642 Irving Street; tel: 664-7225; daily L and D; $
So much flavor for so little cash. This Inner Sunset location is one of several Indian/Pakistani eateries known for its delicious food and low prices. Short on decor but long on spiciness, the chicken vindaloo, tikka masala and tandoori all hit the mark.

Park Superintendents

At the entrance to the McLaren Memorial Rhododendron Dell, just west of the Conservatory of Flowers on John F. Kennedy Drive, you will see a prominent, life-sized statue of "Uncle John" McLaren, the canny park superintendent for 53 years (1890–1943). The statue, erected after his death, is more than a little ironic: the Scotsman notoriously detested statues and deliberately hid those in the park with dense foliage. Though McLaren is the best-known park superintendent, famous for the work he completed during his tenure, he was not the first. That distinction goes to William Hammond Hall from 1871–86.

by Aids. Follow the Woodland Path access ramp, and pass through the redwoods to arrive at the Circle of Friends monument.

Conservatory of Flowers

Walk up Middle Drive East and cross John F. Kennedy Drive to reach the bright-white and beautifully landscaped **Conservatory of Flowers ❾** (tel: 666-7001; www.conservatoryof flowers.org; Tue–Sun 9am–4:30pm; charge except first Tue of month; *see photo, p.72*). Built in the late 1870s, the elegant, glass-domed structure was modeled after the Palm House in

England's Kew Gardens. Vibrantly colored tropical flowers are the main focus of five galleries overflowing with nearly 2,000 plant species. A highland tropics exhibit nurtures a renowned collection of high-altitude orchids amid climbing vines, moss-carpeted rocks, and a profusion of ferns. In the pool-filled aquatic plants exhibit, feast your eyes on carnivorous plants and giant Victoria amazonica water lilies that can reach 6ft (2m) in diameter. The Dahlia Garden decorates the eastern side of the conservatory, while in the spring, 850 varieties of rhododendron bloom in the McLaren Memorial Rhododendron Dell to the west. Walk east on John F. Kennedy Drive to exit the park, turning right on Stanyan left on Haight Street.

Haight-Ashbury History

Filled with grand Victorians and large backyards, Haight-Ashbury began as a suburb that was linked by the Haight Street Cable Railroad to the Financial District. In the housing shortage during World War II, many of these single homes were divided into apartments, which were vacated once the war was over, as families left for the suburbs in the 1950s mass "white flight." Low rents initially attracted the next wave of bohemians that followed the Beats of North Beach. By the mid-1960s, this neighborhood of brightly painted Victorians had filled with head shops, boutiques, bookstores, musicians, and artists. In 1966, at the intersection of Haight and Ashbury streets a young, clean-shaven Jerry Garcia posed with the rest of the Grateful Dead for one of the era's iconic photos, proclaiming the district to be the epicenter of the quickly emerging counterculture. But it was in 1967 when the neighborhood truly gained iconic status, as tens of thousands flocked here for first the "Human Be-In" and then the famous "Summer of Love." The sense of this history is palpable as you walk along Haight Street, particularly from the intersection of Ashbury Street.

HAIGHT-ASHBURY

While "The Haight," as locals call it, is steeped in nostalgia, there are plenty of modern-day hipsters and "hippie" homeless types claiming the neighborhood as their own. The Upper Haight, roughly from Stanyan to Masonic streets, is a mishmash of thrift stores, hip boutiques, cheap eateries, friendly local bars, independent music stores and bookshops. The neighborhood is plagued by persistent panhandlers, and the grungy feel becomes even grittier descending into the Lower Haight (between Divisadero and Webster), but a laid-back atmosphere prevails: most stores open after 11am (or noon on weekends), and the morning traffic rush only starts in the middle of the day.

Haight Street

Stroll east on Haight Street to take in the varied funky shops. **Amoeba Music** ❿ (No. 1855; tel: 831-1200; www. amoebamusic.com; Mon–Sat 10:30am–10pm, Sun 11am–9pm) is a progressive independent music seller housed in a converted bowling alley, with especially fine experimental offerings in rock, hip-hop, electronica, and jazz.

The funky, worker-owned **Red Vic Movie House** ⓫ (No. 1727; tel: 668-3994; www.redvicmoviehouse. com) remains a colorful and dynamic place to watch both classics and unfamiliar fringe titles from comfortable couches.

For a dose of "subversive" literature, pop into **Bound Together Books** ⓬ (No. 1369; tel: 431-8355; www.bound togetherbooks.com; daily 11:30am–7:30pm). This volunteer-run bookstore sells anarchist and other non-traditional literature, and the side of the building features a colorful mural by local artist Susan Greene depicting famous anarchists.

End your tour with a meal at one of the Haight's fun and diverse eateries, such as **Cha Cha Cha**, **Zona Rosa**, **Kan Zaman**, **Squat and Gobble,** and **Magnolia**, see ⓫③, ⓫④, ⓫⑤, ⓫⑥, and ⓫⑦.

Above from far left: painting in the park; elaborate Victorian architecture in Haight-Ashbury; trendy bar in Haight-Ashbury; no mistaking the neighborhood.

Food and Drink

③ CHA CHA CHA
1801 Haight Street; tel: 386-5758; daily L and D; $
Smack dab in the middle of Haight-Ashbury, Cha Cha Cha is a fun place for tapas, Caribbean-inspired entrees, and potent sangria. The crowd is young, hip, and noisy.

④ ZONA ROSA
1797 Haight Street; tel: 668-7717; daily L and D; $; cash only
Craving a burrito but too weary to go all the way to the Mission? This groovy *taquería* is good for a quick bite in a quirky setting. Vegetarian options are particularly popular.

⑤ KAN ZAMAN
1793 Haight Street; tel: 751-9656; daily D only; $
A perennial favorite with local hookah-lovers. Expect a loud, fun night with belly dancers (Thur–Sat) and hookahs filled with fruit-flavored tobacco to smoke at the table while you sit on floor cushions sipping warm spiced wine.

⑥ SQUAT AND GOBBLE
1428 Haight Street; tel: 864-8484; www.squatandgobble.com; daily B and L; $
Yummy and consistent chain with a large open-air patio out back. Pick from sweet and savory crepes served with rosemary garlic potatoes, or from scrambled eggs, sandwiches, and salads, then take your time gobbling, and enjoying the casual, friendly atmosphere.

⑦ MAGNOLIA
1398 Haight Street; tel: 864-7468; www.magnoliapub.com; daily L and D; $$
This brewpub recently underwent a facelift and emerged all grown up, replacing quirky decor with new booths, banquettes, and a long communal table, and upgrading the menu to gastropub fare. And the superb brews that Magnolia built its reputation on? Never fear, those are still in high supply.

10

THE CASTRO

Enjoy truly "good views" from the wooded and steeply sloping Buena Vista Park. Then walk the tidy streets of the rainbow-flag-festooned Castro District, one of the city's most vibrant, diverse, and politically active districts.

Civic Recycling
When the city converted its many cemeteries into parks, workers were ordered to use the unclaimed headstones for the new trails and gutters. Out of respect for the dead, many decided to leave the pieces facing upwards; some of these are still visible today in Buena Vista Park.

DISTANCE 2 miles (3km)
TIME A half-day
START Buena Vista Park
END Castro and 16th streets
POINTS TO NOTE

This tour of the Castro begins at the entrance to Buena Vista Park at Haight Street and Central Avenue. To reach this starting point, take bus 6, 43, 66, or 71. This tour is a good one to do in the afternoon into evening, so consider doing it after walk 11.

The well-groomed Castro, considered by many to be the gay capital of the world, showcases beautifully restored Victorian and Edwardian homes, while draping its thriving nightlife, love of shopping, and political activism in rainbow flags. Along with the Mission *(see pp.79–83)*, it provides San Francisco's political and artistic heartbeat.

BUENA VISTA PARK

Dating from 1867, **Buena Vista Park** ❶ is San Francisco's oldest park. Walk southwest along the steep sidewalk of Buena Vista Avenue West, which clings to the park's edge, passing grand and beautifully restored Victorians. One of these, at No. 737 (not to be confused with the mansion of the same name in Pacific Heights), is the picturesque **Spreckels Mansion** ❷. Built in the late 19th century for sugar magnate Richard Spreckels, the now private residence was also once home to Ambrose Bierce and Jack London.

Buena Vista Avenue West becomes Buena Vista Avenue East, turning sharply northeast. Take the path into the park here for breathtaking downtown views. Then continue on Buena Vista Avenue East, turning right on Buena Vista Terrace, left on 14th Street, and right on Castro Street,

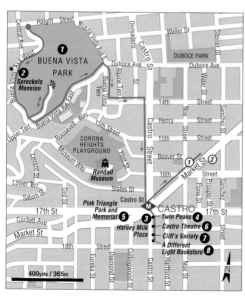

descending to Market Street and the colorful center of the Castro.

THE CASTRO'S HEART

It was only 30 years ago that the Castro shifted from a working-class, Irish Catholic neighborhood to the city's thriving, politically active gay hub, but it is hard now to imagine it any differently. The tightly knit community is safe, well maintained, and filled with friendly eateries, unique shops, and brightly colored Victorians and Edwardians.

Harvey Milk Plaza

At the intersection of Castro and Market streets is **Harvey Milk Plaza** ❸, named for the city's first openly gay Supervisor, elected in 1977, who was assassinated at City Hall with Mayor George Moscone by former Supervisor Dan White. White avoided a murder conviction with the infamous "Twinkie Defense," which claimed a sugar high had reduced White's mental capacity. The lenient sentence provoked enraged protestors to descend on City Hall in the White Night Riot of May 21, 1979, torching the capitol and police cars.

Here also is historic **Twin Peaks** ❹ (401 Castro Street; tel: 864-9470; www.twinpeakstavern.com; Mon–Wed noon–2am, Thur–Sun 8am–2am), a friendly neighborhood tavern and the country's first openly gay bar.

Just to the west of this intersection, an island wedge between Market and 17th streets hosts the **Pink Triangle Park and Memorial** ❺ (http://pink trianglepark.org). The 15,000 or so gays, lesbians, bisexuals, and transgenders who were persecuted during and following the Nazi regime are commemorated here by 15 white-granite pylons inlaid with pink triangles (the symbol once worn by LGBT concentration-camp prisoners) and positioned in the shape of a triangle.

Castro Theatre

Head south on Castro Street for the **Castro Theatre** ❻ (No. 429; tel: 621-6120; www.castrotheatre.com). This ornate yet intimate Spanish Baroque

theater, complete with Art Deco flourishes, was built in 1922 and designated a U.S. National Landmark in 1977. The revival movie house often hosts film festivals, and on special nights a live organist plays on a platform that ascends before the start of the film.

Cliff's Variety

Continue south on Castro. This tightly packed commercial strip largely caters to the gay community and is devoid of retail chains. Instead, look for quirky such as **Cliff's Variety ❼** (479 Castro Street; tel: 431-5365; www.cliffs variety.com; Mon–Fri 8:30am–8pm, Sat 9:30am–8pm, Sun 11am–6pm), a unique hardware store with aisles of tools, craft supplies, fancy-dress outfits, and home-decoration items.

A Different Light Bookstore

At 489 Castro Street is San Francisco's largest gay bookstore, **A Different Light Bookstore ❽** (tel: 431-0891; www.adlbooks.com; daily 10am–10pm, Fri–Sat until 11pm), which stocks a plethora of gay- and lesbian-oriented books, magazines, and newspapers, and also hosts LGBT-related events, from parties to talks and readings.

To end the walk, return to Market Street and turn right to recharge at **Café Flore**, see ⑪①, or **2223 Restaurant**, see ⑪②.

Food and Drink ⑪

① CAFÉ FLORE

2298 Market Street; tel: 621-8579; www.cafeflore.com; daily B, L, and D; $

The diverse crowds that frequent this ever-bustling intersection make this café perfect for people-watching. Order your coffee, *frittata*, or club sandwich at the counter and pounce on a table on the sunny outdoor patio.

② 2223 RESTAURANT

2223 Market Street; tel: 431-0692; www.2223restaurant.com; Mon–Sat D only, Sun Br and D; $$

A chic neighborhood favorite with a warm and festive spirit. Dig into the American comfort-food fare but save room for decadent desserts like the sour cherry bread pudding doused in brandy caramel and red-wine syrup. Also a great bet for Sunday brunch.

THE MISSION DISTRICT

The scruffy Mission District is one of the city's most dynamic, diverse neighborhoods. It is home to a large working-class Latino population and numerous artists and musicians, and is the headquarters for the hip crowd.

The Mission is one of the oldest parts of San Francisco, inhabited by Ohlone Indians for over 2,000 years before Spanish missionaries arrived in the mid-18th century. The area remained remote from the first center of town, Portsmouth Square, until the mid-1850s when large Irish and German working-class immigrant populations settled here. Another wave of development followed the 1906 earthquake,

DISTANCE 2½ miles (4km)
TIME A half-day
START Mission Dolores
END 24th and York streets
POINTS TO NOTE

This district is best explored by day. To reach the starting point by public transport, take bus: 22, 26, or F, or Metro: J, K, L, M, T to Church station.

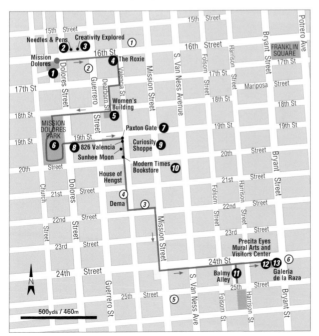

Hot Nightspot

When the sun sets, a boisterous nightlife scene kicks off in the Mission. An über-hip, arty, and alternative twenty- and thirtysomething crowd swarm the noisy local bars to let loose. Among others, Casanova Lounge (527 Valencia Street), Elbo Room (647 Valencia Street), Beauty Bar (2299 Mission Street), and Lazslo (2526 Mission Street) are always busy and open late.

Above from left:
the basilica and
stained glass at
Mission Dolores; an
elaborately tiled dome
on the Mission High
School; candles at
Mission Dolores.

when the neighborhood welcomed
displaced residents and businesses. The
present Latin character of the neighborhood began in the 1940s–1960s
with a growing Mexican community,
who were joined in the 1980s and
1990s by immigrants and refugees
fleeing Central and South America.

MISSION DOLORES

Begin at the intersection of 16th and
Dolores streets for **Mission Dolores**
❶, more formally known as Misión
San Francisco de Asís (3321 16th
Street; tel: 621-8203; www.mission
dolores.org; daily 9am–4pm; donation
suggested). Built in 1776, this narrow
adobe church was sixth in the chain of

21 Spanish missions built along the
California coast. Completed just days
before the signing of the Declaration
of Independence in 1776, it is the
oldest intact building in the city.

Carved Mexican altars stand at the
head of the interior, whose restored
ceiling is decorated with brightly colored Ohlone Indian designs. Above
the vestibule, the original bells still
hang. Outside, in the peaceful cemetery, over 5,000 Native Americans are
buried amidst traditional native trees,
shrubs, flowers, and plants. With them
are some of the first Californians and
pioneers who gave their names to San
Francisco streets, including Don Luis
Antonio Arguello, the first governor of
Alta California under Mexican rule.

16TH STREET

Walk east along arty 16th Street.
Needles & Pens ❷ (No. 3253; tel:
255-1534; www.needles-pens.com;
daily noon–7pm) doubles up as both
an art gallery and purveyor of zines,
locally produced clothing, jewelry,
and music. At No. 3245 sits **Cre-
ativity Explored** ❸ (tel: 863-2108;
www.creativityexplored.org; studio:
Mon–Fri 8:30am–2:30pm, gallery:
Mon–Fri 10am–3pm (Thur until
7pm), Sat 1–6pm), a nonprofit visual-
arts center where artists with devel-
opmental disabilities create, exhibit,
and sell art. Next up is **The Roxie** ❹
(No. 3117; tel: 863-1087; www.roxie.
com), a popular art-house cinema
with a reputation for risk-taking
programs. More documentaries are

Below: statue of
St Francis looking
towards the Mission
Dolores tower.

shown here each year than at any other theater in the country.

THE WOMEN'S BUILDING

For a burrito break, continue on 16th to **Pancho Villa**, see ⑪①, then head south on Valencia Street. Turn right on 17th and then left on Dearborn, a charming residential block with a community garden. Ahead, across 18th Street is the colorful **Women's Building** ❺ (3543 18th Street; tel: 431-1180; www.womensbuilding.org; daily 9am–5pm, additional evening hours vary). The bold and beautiful *Maestra Peace* mural decorates the outside of this "multi-ethnic, multi-cultural, multi-service center for women and girls."

MISSION DOLORES PARK

Head west along 18th Street and turn left on Guerrero Street to grab a coffee and some melt-in-your-mouth pastries at **Tartine Bakery**, see ⑪②, or continue walking to reach the corner of 18th and Dolores and **Mission Dolores Park** ❻. Frisky dogs and energetic ballplayers get their exercise in the lower part of this popular Mission park; higher up, picnickers sun themselves and enjoy the city views. Hike up to the corner near 20th and Church streets, where the vista is most *buena*. Exit the park onto Dolores Street, head east on 19th Street, and then south back onto Valencia Street.

Below: stylish picnicker in Mission Dolores Park.

Food and Drink 🍴

① PANCHO VILLA
3071 16th Street; tel: 864-8840; daily L and D; $
Here it is: the world-renowned San Francisco burrito. Pancho Villa is counter service only, and incredibly inexpensive. Have a late lunch and you will not need dinner. As with most *taquerías*, pass on the refried beans and go with whole or black ones for better flavor and texture.

② TARTINE BAKERY
600 Guerrero Street; tel: 487-2600; www.tartinebakery.com; daily B, L, and D; $
Locals drool over the eclairs, tarts, freshly baked bread and other treats from this small bakery and café. For something more substantial, try a croque-monsieur or a pressed sandwich, accompanied by wine or organic coffee.

Local Style

The neighborhood is home to some exceptional indie clothing designers. Among them are Dema (1038 Valencia Street; tel: 206-0500; www.godemago. com; Mon–Fri 11am–7pm, Sat noon–7pm, Sun noon–6pm), House of Hengst (924 Valencia Street; tel: 642-0841; www. houseofhengst.com; Mon–Sat noon–7pm, Sun noon–6pm), Minnie Wilde (3266 21st Street; tel: 642-9453; www.minnie wilde.com; Mon–Fri noon–7pm, Sat 11am–7pm, Sun 11am–5pm), and Sunhee Moon (3167 16th Street; tel: 355-1800; www.sunhee moon.com; Mon–Fri noon–7pm, Sat–Sun noon–6pm).

Below: Latino food.

VALENCIA STREET

As the bohemian center of the Mission, Valencia Street is filled with great book-stores, quirky shops, hip bars, and internet cafés. Walk south on Valencia for quirky collectibles. **Paxton Gate** ❼ (No. 824; tel: 824-1872; www.paxton-gate.com; Mon–Fri noon–7pm, Sat–Sun 11am–7pm) hosts an unconventional collection of items inspired by gardens and the natural sciences, including tools, taxidermy, and tea. Next door is **826 Valencia** ❽ (tel: 642-5914; www.826valencia.org; daily noon–6pm), a youth literary center co-founded by local literary talent Dave Eggers. Somewhat bizarrely, 826 Valenica also doubles as a Pirate Supply Store, filled with eye patches, message bottles, spyglasses, and other pirate paraphernalia.

Across the street is the **Curiosity Shoppe** ❾ (No. 855; tel: 671-5384; www.curiosityshoppeonline.com; Wed–Sat 11am–7pm, Sun noon–6pm) brimming with "crafts, kits, and curios for the creatively inclined." Whimsical knick-knacks such as porcelain keys and woodland-inspired carvings are offered along with nifty do-it-yourself guides explaining how to build radio receivers and mechanical music boxes.

Modern Times Bookstore ❿ (888 Valencia Street; tel: 282-9246; www. mtbs.com; Mon–Sat 10am–9pm, Sun 11am–6pm) pulls in politically inclined bibliophiles with its offerings related to globalization, politics, and media, and also has a wide selection of literature concerning all things Latino.

MISSION STREET

Turn left on 22nd Street. If you need a break at this point, join the local artists and musicians at **Revolution Café**, see ⑪③. Turn right on Mission, passing choice dinner spots such as **Foreign Cinema**, see ⑪④, and casually hip cafés. Mission Street's numerous Art Deco marquees speak of a more prosperous time, but the street is still rich in culture and artistic energy. Full of discount stores, Mexican grocery stores, and late-night spots, it is a vibrant neighborhood, albeit rather less salubrious after dark. For a change of taste, pick up a slice of something sweet at **Mission Pie**, see ⑪⑤.

24TH STREET

Turn east on 24th Street, known as *El Corazón de la Misión* (the Heart of the Mission). The Latino culture for which the Mission is famous is especially evident in this area: in particular, the stretch of 24th Street from Mission to

Folsom is lined with trees and peppered with *taquerías*, mural-adorned alleys, and art organizations.

Balmy Alley

Turn right onto **Balmy Alley** ⓫, where murals depicting scenes from life in the Mission or in Central American villages cover almost every wall. Murals throughout the Mission express its political consciousness as well as a deep connection to *La Raza* (the race, or the people). Guided tours of the murals in this area are conducted by the **Precita Eyes Mural Arts and Visitors Center** ⓬ (2981 24th Street; tel: 285-2287; www.precitaeyes.org; center: Mon–Fri 10am–5pm, Sat 10am–4pm, Sun noon–4pm, tours:

check website for details of walks currently offered; charge). It also offers lots of information about the Mission's murals and a store that sells lovely gifts and art supplies.

Galería de la Raza

Further along 24th Street is **Galería de la Raza** ⓭ (No. 2857; tel: 826-8009; www.galeriadelaraza.org; Tue 1–7pm, Wed–Sat noon–6pm (but call to confirm hours); free), a mixed space for art and activism that celebrates Chicano and Latino art and culture. Founded in 1970, it is largely considered the most important Chicano art center in the country. You can now end your tour with a satisfying meal at **St Francis Fountain**, see ⑥.

Above from far left: detail of one of the many murals in this part of town; the Foreign Cinema, on Mission Street.

Food and Drink

③ REVOLUTION CAFÉ

3248 22nd Street; tel: 642-0474; daily B, L, and D; $

This French-style café is a friendly gathering place for artists, musicians, and other bohemian types, who enjoy chatting in the down-to-earth atmosphere and, some nights, listening to live classical and jazz music while drinking wine and beer. Indoor and outdoor seating available.

④ FOREIGN CINEMA

2534 Mission Street; tel: 648-7600; daily D; $$$

"Dinner and a movie" gets a new spin at this popular industrial-chic eatery with innovative California cuisine. Diners can choose to sit inside or dine in the heated outdoor courtyard, where films are screened nightly on a concrete wall.

⑤ MISSION PIE

2901 Mission Street; tel: 282-1500; www.missionpie.com; daily B, L, and D; $

Get your pie fix from morning to night at this corner café and bakery, whose mission is to use produce from local farms, and to encourage healthy and sustainable lives. The menu is limited to a few daily options, but whether it is yummy banana cream pie, walnut, or strawberry rhubarb, a slice is sure to bring a smile to your face.

⑥ ST FRANCIS FOUNTAIN

2801 24th Street; tel: 826-4200; daily B, L, and D; $$

Family-owned since 1918, this pink-walled 1940s-style soda fountain serves up ice cream and house-made candy as well as hearty breakfasts, sandwiches, and daily specials, with plenty of attention paid to vegetarian options.

FORT MASON AND THE MARINA

This walk involves no hills and, in the main, skirts along the sea-breeze-swept waterfront of the Marina's northern boundary. It takes you from old Fort Mason to the Palace of Fine Arts before winding inland to reach Chestnut Street, the Marina's classy commercial thoroughfare.

Above: drinks at Greens *(see opposite).*

Park HQ
Fort Mason houses the headquarters of the Golden Gate National Recreational Area (GGNRA; www.nps.gov/goga), a 74,000-acre (29,947-hectare), a national park that stretches across 28 miles (45km) of coastline in San Francisco, Marin, and San Mateo counties. It includes major attractions such as Alcatraz, the Presidio, Muir Woods, and the Marin Headlands.

DISTANCE 3 miles (5km)
TIME A half-day
START Fort Mason
END Chestnut Street
POINTS TO NOTE

From the start of Marina Boulevard, the wave organ is a 1-mile (1.6km) round trip. The tour begins at Marina Boulevard and Laguna Street at the entrance to Fort Mason (Metro: F to the Embarcadero and Stockton Street; bus: 10, 15).

Dating back to the Civil War period, Fort Mason is now the north shore's culture capital; its piers and buildings host all manner of performances and recreational activities. The Marina neighborhood in which it is found is popular with young professionals, who make good money in the Financial District and pack out the local bars at the weekend.

FORT MASON

A military base for over 200 years, the 13-acre (5-hectare) waterfront of **Fort Mason ❶** (tel: 441-3400; www.fort mason.org) once served as an embarkation point for troops and supplies headed to the Pacific during the World War II and the Korean conflict. In 1977, Fort Mason was transformed into a cultural center, and the Mission Revival buildings house nonprofit organizations and host 15,000 different kinds of event each year.

Center Highlights

The lofty, light-filled **SFMOMA Artists Gallery** (Fort Mason Building A; tel: 441-4777; www.sfmoma.org; Tue–Sat 11:30am–5:30pm; free) shows sculpture, painting, photography, and mixed-media work from Northern California artists, and offers an innovative art-rental program. Building D houses the **Magic Theater**, which has premiered works by Pulitzer Prize-winners Sam Shepard and David Mamet and innovative pieces by emerging playwrights.

The small permanent collection at **Museo Italo-Americano ❷** (Fort Mason Building C; tel: 673-2200; www.museoitaloamericano.org; Mon by appointment, Tue–Sun noon–4pm; free) features paintings, sculptures, photographs, and works on paper by

prominent Italian and Italian-American artists.

Pop into **Greens**, see ⑪①, for tasty herbivore food with harbor views; alternatively, tote to-go purchases from their take-out counter for a picnic on Marina Green.

YACHT HARBOR TO THE WAVE ORGAN

Exit Fort Mason through the western parking lot, hugging the coast past **Gaslight Cove** ❸ (also known as the East Harbor), one of the Marina's two yacht harbors. Follow the shoreline promenade along the long and lovely **Marina Green** ❹, sandwiched between the bay and Marina Boulevard. The flat, scenic stretch in an otherwise hilly city is a favorite of walkers, joggers, picnickers, and kite-fliers.

The Wave Organ

Veer right onto Yacht Road and wrap around the West Harbor, passing the Saint Francis and Golden Gate yacht clubs. At the end of the rocky jetty is the **Wave Organ** ❺, an acoustic sculpture comprising 25 organ pipes. Sea water swelling in and out causes the pipes to emit subtle tones. Try to visit at high tide to hear them at their best. Enjoy picturesque views of the Golden Gate Bridge, then retrace your steps and cross Marina Boulevard.

EXPLORATORIUM

It is easy to spend hours among the hundreds of hands-on exhibits at the fascinating and kid-friendly **Exploratorium** ❻ (3601 Lyon Street; tel: 561-0360; www.exploratorium.edu; Tue–Sun 10am–5pm; charge, 1st Wed of month free). Conceived by the American physicist Frank Oppenheimer, this museum of science, art,

Above from far left: boats in the marina; walking the dog on the beach, part of the GGNRA; child's play at the Exploratorium.

Below: acrobatics at the Magic Theater.

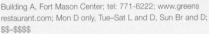

Food and Drink

① GREENS
Building A, Fort Mason Center; tel: 771-6222; www.greens restaurant.com; Mon D only, Tue–Sat L and D, Sun Br and D; $$–$$$$
This airy, upscale vegetarian restaurant is located in a former army warehouse with a beautiful bayside setting. It serves savory fare that even non-veggies rave about, from filled filo pastries to mesquite-grilled vegetable brochettes. The Saturday-evening prix-fixe menu is a relative bargain. Reservations are essential, but not for its take-out counter, Greens to Go, which is open all day.

and human perception explores topics as varied as physics, computers, biology, visual perception, language, and memory. In the bizarre Tactile Dome exhibit (extra charge; reservations recommended), you crawl, climb, squeeze, and grope through a pitch-black maze of materials, designed to develop awareness of your sense of touch.

PALACE OF FINE ARTS

The **Palace of Fine Arts** ❼ was built for the 288-day Panama-Pacific International Exposition of 1915, a world's fair that celebrated the completion of the Panama Canal and (unofficially) San Francisco's rebound from the 1906 disaster. Designed by Bernard Maybeck, the stunning Beaux Arts structure, with massive colonnades and imposing rotunda, was originally made of plaster and was reconstructed out of concrete in the 1960s. Today it hosts occasional events. Take a break on the bench-lined lawns, watching swans swim across the mirror-like lagoon, then walk south on Baker Street to turn left on Bay Street, right on Broderick Street, and finally left on Chestnut Street.

CHESTNUT STREET

Chestnut Street ❽ is the main commercial thoroughfare of the Marina District, and caters to a fairly homogeneous crowd of well-to-do young professionals who frequent the upscale restaurants, mainstream home-and-beauty retailers, glossy boutiques, and happening singles bars.

Above: details and views of the Palace of Fine Arts, dating to 1915.

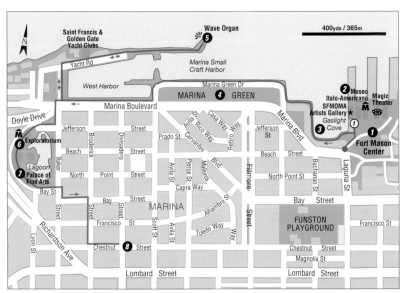

GOLDEN GATE PROMENADE

This straight seaside ramble runs along the restored tidal marshland of Crissy Field to the historic Fort Point at the base of the Golden Gate Bridge. Continue along the bridge for stellar views back over the city.

Perhaps the most photographed bridge in the world, the iconic Golden Gate Bridge, painted in "International Orange," is certainly one of the world's most famous. Numerous movies have featured it as a backdrop or contain scenes filmed on the bridge *(see p. 22)*. No trip to the city is complete without at least a visit to its base if not a walk or drive across it.

GOLDEN GATE PROMENADE

Begin at Yacht Road, north of Marina Boulevard. Head northwards along the bayfront promenade, enjoying stiff, salty breezes as you ramble along **Crissy Field ❶**, a restored tidal marshland

DISTANCE 2½ miles (4km)
TIME 2 hours
START Crissy Field
END Fort Point
POINTS TO NOTE

Fort Point is closed Mon–Thur. A wide, fully accessible trail is convenient for wheelchairs and strollers. For a quieter and less blustery walk, do this tour in the early morning, as the wind generally picks up by midday. To get within four blocks of the tour's starting point, take the 30 bus to Broderick and Jefferson streets. To return downtown from Fort Point, take the 28 bus to the Marina and transfer to the 30.

Playing in the Wind

Swimming in the bay is dangerous because of strong under-currents, but wind sports are very popular. Two companies that offer lessons in the vicinity are Kite Wind Surf (tel (toll-free): 877-521-9463; www.kitewind surf.com) and Board Sports School (tel: 315-1224; www.board sportschool.com).

Above: the bridge in the mist. Left: doggy fun in the sand.

Birthday Celebration
When the city celebrated the Golden Gate's 50th anniversary, some 300,000 admirers made their way onto the bridge. It was the heaviest load the bridge had experienced in its history, and onlookers were shocked as the structure visibly sank beneath their weight.

with 22 acres (9 hectares) of dunes. It was once the airfield of the Presidio army base, and was named after military aviator Major Dana H. Crissy. With its flat, tidy trail and great views, it is a popular spot with locals and visitors alike, who come to walk, run, and bike, or simply to relax with a picnic and watch the expert windsurfing and parasailing taking place at the East Beach.

Crissy Field is also part of the 1,491-acre (603-hectare) **Presidio** (bordered by Lyon Street and West Pacific Avenue; tel: 561-4323; www.nps.gov/prsf; free). A military post for over 200 years, Presidio today is a shoreline park boasting beaches, cliffs, woods, historical sites, a golf course, a lake, 14 miles (23km) of paved roads, and 11 miles (18km) of hiking trails.

FORT POINT

At the intersection of Long Avenue and Marine Drive are the administrative offices of Fort Point (Marine Drive; tel: 556-1693; www.nps.gov/fopo; Fri–Sun 10am–5pm). Here you may take a break at the **Warming Hut**, see ⓘⓘ, and smooth your windblown hair. Follow Marine Drive to its end to reach **Fort Point ❷**, a massive structure variously known as the "the pride of the Pacific," "the Gibraltar of the West Coast," and "one of the most perfect models of masonry in America."

Fort Point is significant for its military and maritime history as well as its architecture. Built between 1853 and 1861, during the height of Gold Rush, Fort Point was designed to stand sentry and protect against foreign attack on San Francisco Bay.

Highlights
A collection of exhibits and information relating to the fort's construction is found on the first floor. The floor above contains exhibits on the Fort Point lighthouses, African-American

Misleading Name

Despite its name, the Golden Gate Bridge is actually painted a burned orange. The original plan was to paint the approach pylons on either side of the bridge gold, but no one ever took that idea seriously. The chief engineer, who thought most bridges, rather boringly, were painted gray, had suggested a silvery aluminum color, much like the color chosen for the 1936 Bay Bridge, though the final color is thought to be the responsibility of Irving Morrow, the bridge district's consulting architect, who was also responsible for the elegant Art Deco design. Known as "International Orange," the hue is a unique blend of orange and black paint that does look rather golden when the sun sets behind it.

Buffalo Soldiers of the Civil War, and the roles of women in war. On the third floor, look for a photo exhibit of the Golden Gate Bridge's construction, for which Fort Point was the headquarters. Films also recount the construction of the fort and its history from 1776 through World War II.

Free 30-minute tours (call for times) leave from the front entrance, and special programs are offered, such as a demonstration of how a Napoleon 12-pounder cannon would be loaded and fired during a Civil War artillery drill.

GOLDEN GATE BRIDGE

Fort Point offers a unique vantage point from its location beneath the **Golden Gate Bridge ❸** (www.goldengate bridge.org). Work on the suspension bridge started on January 5, 1933, and was finished on May 27, 1937. More than 100,000 tons of steel were used, and its construction involved 25 mil-

lion person-hours and the accidental death of 11 workers. It was the first bridge in the world to experiment with one-way toll collection. Follow the signs to climb the bluffs to the bridge's toll plaza. The walk across the bridge is 1¼ miles (3km), and pedestrian access to the bridge is permitted during daylight hours only. (Note: there is no public-transport stop to return to the city on the Marin side on weekdays; pedestrians and cyclists share the same sidewalks.)

Above: the fenced-off sidewalk is shared by pedestrians and cyclists.

> ## Food and Drink 🍴
> ① **WARMING HUT**
> Presidio Building 983; tel: 561-3040;
> daily 9am–5pm; $
> The bright café is the perfect place to rest and recharge after a wind-blown walk along Crissy Field. Get toasty with a hot cup of coffee, fresh pastries, sandwiches, and other offerings with an emphasis on fresh, organic ingredients. Then browse the store selling books and gifts with an environmental theme.

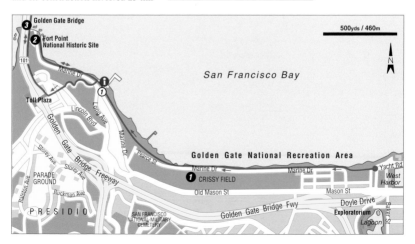

BERKELEY

Visit the liberal, diverse city and handsome university campus that became synonymous in the 1960s with the student Free Speech Movement, flower power, and student protests against the Vietnam War.

DISTANCE 3 miles (5km)
TIME A full day
START/END Downtown Berkeley
POINTS TO NOTE

The distance noted above does not include detours to the Rose Garden, Lawrence Hall of Science, Botanical Gardens, or Tilden Park; the last three require a car or public transport for access. For lunch at Chez Panisse, call ahead for reservations.

North Berkeley Hills
Detour to the North Berkeley Rose Garden (Euclid Avenue between Eunice Street and Bay View Place) for gorgeous views. Cut north across Memorial Glade to the campus's North Gate, and wait for the 65 bus or walk north half of a mile on Euclid. Just blocks off campus into the North Berkeley hills, the atmosphere changes dramatically: the noisy and hectic hubbub dies away, and winding streets grow wooded and peacefully residential.

Across the bay from San Francisco is the university town of Berkeley. Since the Free Speech Movement in 1964, it has been a hotbed of political activism. The university campus is a sprawling temple to education, full of earnest students and Nobel Prize-winning professors.

Food and Drink 🍴

① FREE SPEECH MOVEMENT CAFÉ
Berkeley campus (at Moffitt Library); daily 8am–2am; $
Students line up between classes for coffee and black-bottom muffins at this animated campus café, then return for study-lunches over salads and panini. Getting a table can be difficult because the students camp out for hours, but try to snag a table on the large outdoor patio.

UNIVERSITY OF CALIFORNIA, BERKELEY CAMPUS

To reach the University Campus, take BART to the Downtown Berkeley station and then the Shattuck and Center streets exit. Turn right down Center and then left on Oxford Street to find the western entrance of the **University of California, Berkeley**. Just a bit farther north, at Oxford Street and University Avenue, pick up campus maps at **Visitor Services ❶** (University Hall, Room 101; tel: 510-642-5216; Mon–Fri 8:30am–4:30pm). Enter the campus through the West Gate's semicircular lawn and follow the long driveway onto campus. You will pass the 3-acre (1-hectare) **Valley Life Sciences Building** on the right, which is one of the largest academic facilities in the nation.

Campus Libraries
Continuing east, you will pass the open-stack **Moffitt Library** and the adjacent **Free Speech Movement Café**, see 🍴①, on your left. Past the library, climb the staircase to the stunning Beaux Arts **Doe Library ❷**. Inside this main campus library, the lovely Morrison Library Reading Room to the right offers comfortable

couches to sink into and rest; up the marble staircase (with hollows on each step worn down from years of student traffic) is the bright, airy, and cavernous North Reading Room, filled with long tables and canopied by an ornate coffered ceiling. In a nearby room hangs Emanuel Gottlieb Leutze's *Washington Rallying the Troops at Mon- mouth* (1854).

Back outside, you can choose to head to North Berkeley Rose Garden off campus *(see margin tip, left)* or turn right and walk along grassy **Memorial Glade ❸**, a memorial to the alumni, faculty, and staff who served in World War II, and a favorite spot among students for sunbathing, napping, reading, and Frisbee-tossing.

Sather Tower

Turn right and walk towards the spindly **Sather Tower ❹**, better-known as the Campanile. Built in 1914, the clock tower was modeled on the tower in Venice's Piazza San Marco, and named after a school benefactor, Jane K. Sather. The 61-bell carillon at the top of the tower sings out several times each day, and plays a dirge on the last day of classes before finals. Take the elevator (charge) to the top for wonderful views of the campus and bay. Then, you can choose to take a detour by bus to Berkeley Botanical Garden and Lawrence Hall of Science *(see below)* or walk southeast from Sather Tower, crossing the car-access road south of LeConte and Birge halls and hopping down the stairway. Cross Strawberry Creek and follow the path

up around Faculty Glade. Pass Hertz Hall on the left and exit the campus onto Bancroft Way at College Avenue.

Berkeley Botanical Garden and Lawrence Hall of Science

To reach the Berkeley Botanical Garden or Lawrence Hall of Science up in Berkeley's hills, head north from Sather Tower to the Hearst Mining Circle just opposite Evans Hall, where the Hill Shuttle (the H Line) departs every half-hour (Mon–Fri 7:40am–6:10pm).

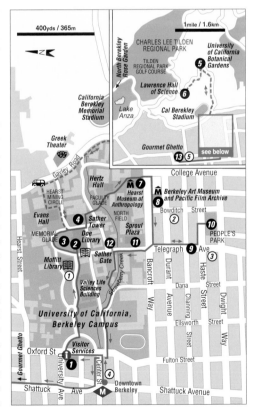

Above from left:
the Sather Tower;
mural at the
People's Park.

High Fliers
UC Berkeley attracts
exceptional faculty
staff, with 20 full-time
faculty members
having won the Nobel
Prize over the years.
In addition to the
honor and recognition
accompanied by
the prize, the school's
laureates receive
a choice bonus:
reserved parking
on campus. Look
for parking spaces
labeled 'NL' north
of LeConte Hall,
which sits just east
of the Campanile.

Chocolate Factory
Berkeley might be full
of people hungry for
knowledge, but if your
hunger is for some-
thing sweeter hop in
a cab to the Sharffen
Berger chocolate
factory (914 Heinz
Avenue, Berkeley:
tel: 800-930-4528;
www.scharffenberger.
com; Mon–Sat
10am–6pm, Sun
10am–5pm; free) for a
one-hour presentation
on chocolate making
and factory tour.

The **University of California Botanical Gardens** ❺ (200 Centennial Drive; tel: 510-643-2755; http://botanicalgarden.berkeley.edu; daily 9am–5pm, closed 1st Tue of month; charge, 1st Thur of month free) packs an amazing array of native California and exotic plant species into gardens high in the Berkeley hills. Another stop on the H Line is the **Lawrence Hall of Science** ❻ (tel: 510-642-5132; www.lhs.berkeley.edu; daily 10am–5pm; charge), which offers engaging hands-on exhibits related to maths and science. Kids also enjoy climbing on the giant whale outside,

and everyone oohs and aahs over gorgeous views of San Francisco and the bay from the snack bar and parking lot. Return to campus and make your way back past the Sather Tower and on to Bancroft Way *(see p.91 for directions)*.

Hearst Museum of Anthropology
The bijou **Hearst Museum of Anthropology** ❼ (Kroeber Hall at Bancroft Way; tel: 510-643-7649; http://hearstmuseum.berkeley.edu/; term-time only: Wed–Sat 10am–4:30pm, Sun noon–4pm; free) can only display a tiny fraction of the 3.8 million artifacts in its collection at any one time. However,

---

Food and Drink

② **TOP DOG**
2534 Durant Avenue; tel: 510-843-5967; www.topdoghotdogs.com; daily L and D; $
Open until 2am, Top Dog has been satisfying the post-partying munchies of students for decades. Luckily, the *kielbasa*, bratwurst, and other simple and specialty dogs are just as delicious earlier in the day.

③ **CAFÉ INTERMEZZO**
2442 Telegraph Avenue; tel: 510-849-4592; daily L and D; $
This little salad, sandwich, and soup joint is a great healthy bang for your buck, and becomes a regular for most Berkeley students with generous portions, affordable prices, and a completely relaxed atmosphere. Grab a window seat to people-watch the colorful characters on Telegraph Avenue and gnaw on the huge hunk of bread thrown in with every meal.

④ **JUPITER**
2181 Shattuck Avenue; tel: 510-843-8277; www.jupiterbeer. com; daily L and D; $$
A two-story brewpub with large tables, wood-fired pizzas, gourmet focaccia sandwiches, and great ambience. The fantastic brick-walled outdoor patio is lined with trees and often hosts live jazz and folk music. Some 30 beers are on tap, including house brews and other regional craft beers, along with wine and pomegranate cider.

⑤ **CHEZ PANISSE**
1517 Shattuck Avenue, Berkeley; tel: 510-548-5525; www.chezpanisse.com; Mon–Sat D only; $$$
The birthplace of California cuisine, founded by Alice Waters, who pioneered the use of local, seasonal ingredients. Courses are fixed by the chef, with two seatings each night. There is also a café that serves lunch.

exhibits are regularly changed, and there's a great museum store.

BERKELEY ART MUSEUM AND PACIFIC FILM ARCHIVE

Turn right on Bancroft Way for the **Berkeley Art Museum and Pacific Film Archive** ❽ (No. 2626; tel: 510-642-0808; www.bampfa.berkeley.edu; Wed–Sun 11am–5pm, Thur until 7pm; charge except 1st Thur of the month). This collection of over 13,000 artworks (the largest university art museum in the U.S.) includes works by Mark Rothko, Jackson Pollock, and Albert Bierstadt. Within the complex, the **Pacific Film Archive** offers daily screenings pulled from a pool of 10,000 movies, including international classics, Soviet silents, rare animation, and the largest collection of Japanese films outside of Japan.

TELEGRAPH AVENEUE

Continue down Bancroft a few more blocks and turn left on **Telegraph Avenue** ❾, a counterculture landmark that bustles with students, panhandlers, and street vendors hawking tie-dyed shirts and an impressive array of beaded and precious-metal jewelry. Telegraph is rife with eateries cheap enough for student budgets; try trusty **Top Dog**, see ⑪②, or **Café Intermezzo**, see ⑪③. East of Telegraph and bordered by Haste Street and Dwight Way is **People's Park** ❿, the site of a legendary student-police confrontation in the late 1960s, now largely a hangout for the city's homeless population.

SPROUL PLAZA AND SATHER GATE

Retrace your steps on Telegraph and cross Bancroft Way to re-enter the campus at **Sproul Plaza** ⓫. This is where the Free Speech Movement kicked off in 1964; today, the busy plaza is frequently lined with student group tables and filled with demonstrators, eating and lounging students, and the oddball entertainer or evangelist.

Donated by Jane K. Sather in memory of her late husband Peder Sather, **Sather Gate** ⓬ was once the end of Telegraph Avenue, a turning point for trolleys from Oakland, and the university's southern entrance. Now the landmark stands between Sproul Plaza and a bridge over Strawberry Creek.

Turn left at Sather Gate and walk downhill, keeping Strawberry Creek on your right. Look out for and then cross the wooden bridge with a tree growing out of the center, then bear left on the path ahead to exit the campus.

Food Options

Cross Oxford onto Center, then turn right on Shattuck Avenue. If you are hungry, break at **Jupiter**, see ⑪④, or continue north on Shattuck to reach **Chez Panisse**, see ⑪⑤, for California cuisine at its best. Alternatively, turn right on Vine and then right on Walnut to find the heart of **Gourmet Ghetto** ⓭ and more tasty options. Then head back to the Downtown Berkeley BART station on Shattuck to return to San Francisco.

Green Spaces

The northeast parts of Berkeley are marked by beautifully wooded hills, including the vast Tilden Park (entrances off Canon Drive, Shasta Road, or South Park Drive, all off Grizzly Peak Boulevard, Berkeley; tel: 510-843-2137; www.ebparks.org/parks/tilden; daily 5am–10pm; free). Well worth an afternoon detour, Tilden features numerous trails and ample places for picnics. Hike on Nimitz Way, stroll around Lake Anza (tel: 510-843-2137), admire California native plants at the botanic garden (tel: 510-841-8732), or hit a bucket of balls at the 18-hole public golf course (tel: 510-848-7373). Children enjoy the merry-go-round and small steam train (tel: 510-548-6100). On weekends, take the 67 bus from the Downtown Berkeley BART station, which runs every half-hour. On weekdays, it only goes as far as the Canon Drive and Shasta Road entrance.

DIRECTORY

A user-friendly alphabetical listing of practical information, plus hand-picked hotels and restaurants, clearly organized by area, to suit all budgets and tastes, along with suggestions for evening entertainment.

A–Z	96
ACCOMMODATIONS	108
RESTAURANTS	114
ENTERTAINMENT	120

A

AGE RESTRICTIONS

You must be over 21 years of age to be able to drink legally in San Francisco. The minimum legal age for smoking is 18 years old. Expect to have to show I.D. to buy alcohol in bars, clubs, and restaurants.

C

CHILDREN

One of the great things about traveling with children in San Francisco is that many of the city's attractions are suitable for people of all ages. A stroll across the Golden Gate Bridge, exploring the markets of Chinatown, cresting a hill aboard a cable-car, or zigzagging down legendary Lombard Street are all crowd-pleasers for young and old alike. San Francisco is a very kid-friendly city with an abundance of state-of-the-art playgrounds, restaurants that offer children's menus (and often crayons), bathrooms equipped with changing tables for babies, and lots of wide open spaces for running around in. Most hotels allow children to stay in parents' rooms at no additional charge (though there is usually an age limit for this) and will provide a rollaway bed or portable crib as needed.

Good internet resources for family travel include: www.familytravelforum.com, www.familytravelnetwork.com, and www.travelingwithyourkids.com.

CLIMATE

San Francisco weather can change significantly from hour to hour and between neighborhoods. Springs are pleasantly warm and sunny (average high in April 63°F/17°C; low 50°F/10°C), while summers can be overcast and typified by fog (average high in July 66°F/19°C; low 54°F/12°C). Come September and October, the summer chill is replaced with beautifully mild, sunny days (average high in September 70°F/21°C; low 56°F/14°C). Rainstorms (no snow) appear in December and January, though crisp, sunny days offer breaks from the damp and dreary ones (average high in January 56°F/14°C; low 46°F/8°C).

CLOTHING

Plan for variable weather and bring clothes that can be layered, as well as comfortable walking shoes: the city's hills are hard to climb in high heels. A raincoat and sturdy umbrella are vital for winter months, when windy rainstorms are common. The city's casual, come-as-you-are vibe means jeans, T-shirts, and tennis shoes are ubiquitous on streets and in many restaurants and entertainment venues. However, fancier eateries and nightclubs warrant something a bit smarter.

CRIME AND SAFETY

As a major city, San Francisco does see some crime, and travelers should exercise good common sense, avoiding

seedy neighborhoods and being cautious about walking around alone and at night. Avoid parks after dark. Neighborhoods with less safe reputations include the Tenderloin, Civic Center, Western Addition, the Lower Haight, the Mission south of 24th Street, South of Market above 5th Street, and Bayview districts.

CUSTOMS

Adult visitors staying longer than 72 hours may bring the following into the country duty-free: 1 liter of wine or liquor; 100 cigars (non-Cuban), or 3lbs of tobacco, or 200 cigarettes; and gifts valued under $100.

Absolutely no food (even in cans) or plants are permissible. Visitors may also arrive and depart with up to $10,000 currency without needing to declare it. For the most up-to-date information on what you can bring with you, refer to the U.S. Customs and Border Protection website (www.cbp.gov).

D

DISABLED TRAVELERS

The city's topography presents obvious challenges to those who have mobility problems, but San Francisco is relatively "disabled-friendly."

Societies that can provide useful information include **MossRehab** (tel: 800-2255-6677; www.mossresourcenet.org) and the Society for Accessible Travel & Hospitality (SATH; tel: 212-447-7284; www.sath.org).

E

ELECTRICITY

Electricity in the U.S. is 110 Volts, 60 Hertz A.C. Flat-blade, two-pronged plugs are typical, though some points have three-pronged sockets. Most foreign appliances need a transformer and/or plug adapter.

EMBASSIES/CONSULATES

Australia: tel: 536-1970; www.dfat.gov.au.
Canada: tel: 834-3180; www.sanfrancisco.gc.ca.
Ireland: tel: 392-4214; www.irelandemb.org.
New Zealand: tel: 399-1255; www.nzemb.org.
South Africa: tel: 202-232-4400; www.saembassy.org.
U.K.: tel: 617-1300; www.britainusa.com/sf.
Details for other embassies and consulates can be found in the Yellow Pages.

EMERGENCY NUMBERS

For ambulance, fire, or police, dial 911; if you need to call from a public phone, no coins needed.

F

FESTIVALS

January
Dr Martin Luther King Jr.'s Birthday Celebrations. Events across town.

Green Issues
With an extensive recycling program, a bike-riding population, and countless campaigns to "green" the city by planting trees and native species on its rooftops and public spaces, San Francisco has rightly developed a reputation for being an eco-friendly city. But as much as it tries, it is also a densely populated metropolitan area that carries the inevitable environmental concerns, ranging from air quality to water shortages. San Francisco's greatest threat lies just below the surface in the network of seismic faults that occasionally jolt the city and can cost lives and millions of dollars' worth of damage.

February

Chinese New Year Parade. One of the largest events of its kind outside Asia. www.chineseparade.com.

March

San Francisco Garden Show. Acres of extraordinary gardens, seminars, and shopping. www.gardenshow.com.

St Patrick's Day Parade. A full day of celebration at Civic Center and one of the longest-running parades in the U.S.

April

Cherry Blossom Festival. Two weekends of Japanese art, music, and food. www.nccbf.org.

San Francisco International Film Festival. www.sfiff.org.

May

Bay to Breakers. A 7½-mile (11km) footrace. Participants don outrageous costumes. www.baytobreakers.com.

Carnaval. Hispanic Mission district comes alive with floats, dancers, and Latino music. www.carnavalsf.com.

June

Haight Street Fair. One of the city's wildest street fairs. www.haightstreetfair.org.

North Beach Festival. The city's oldest street fair. www.sfnorthbeach.org/festival.

San Francisco Pride Celebration and Parade. A weekend of events including a huge Sunday parade. www.sfpride.org.

Stern Grove Midsummer Music Festival. Classical, jazz, world music, and picnics (June–Aug). www.sterngrove.org.

July

Fourth of July Waterfront Festival. Independence Day celebrations feature live music and firework displays over the bay. www.fishermanswharf.org.

Jewish Film Festival. www.sfjff.org.

August

Nihonmachi Street Fair. A celebration of the Bay Area's Asian- and Pacific-American communities. www.nihonmachistreetfair.org.

September

Comedy Day. Free stand-up in Golden Gate Park. www.comedyday.com.

Free Opera in the Park. "Greatest hits" performed by the San Francisco Opera in Golden Gate Park. Free. www.sfgate.com/chronicle/events/opera.

San Francisco Blues Festival. One of America's largest blues festivals. www.sfblues.com.

San Francisco Fringe Festival. Independent theater, performance art, and comedy held in various venues. www.sffringe.org.

San Francisco Shakespeare Festival. Free Shakespeare in the Park and programs for youngsters. www.sfshakes.org.

October

Fleet Week. Fisherman's Wharf welcomes the U.S. Navy. Highlights include the Blue Angels airshow. www.military.com/fleetweek .

Hardly Strictly Bluegrass Festival. Some of the biggest names in bluegrass, country, and rockabilly perform free for three days in Golden Gate Park. www.strictlybluegrass.com.

November

Christmas Tree Lighting Ceremonies. The city lights up in Union Square on the Saturday after Thanksgiving.

Dia de los Muertos. The Mexican Day of the Dead is celebrated with drummers, altars, and dancing skeletons. www.dayofthedeadsf.org.

Green Festival. The largest environment expo in the world.

December

Festival of Lights. The lighting of a Hanukkah menorah in Union Square.

SFNYE (San Francisco New Year's Eve). City-wide celebration with live music and fireworks.

FURTHER READING

From Frogs to a Falcon

San Francisco's literary heritage kicked off in the Gold Rush years, with Mark Twain penning *The Celebrated Jumping Frog of Calaveras County*, 1865. In Oakland, "Prince of the Oyster Pirates" Jack London (*The Call of the Wild*, 1903) bought his first sloop at the still-standing First and Last Chance Saloon on Jack London Square. Oakland remembers Gertrude Stein rather less fondly; she wrote of Oakland, "There is no there there." Back across the Bay, Dashiell Hammett (*The Maltese Falcon*, 1930) spun hardboiled detectives based on his Pinkerton detective days.

Beats and Beyond

In the mid-1950s North Beach became Beat Central, attracting Jack Kerouac (author of Beat manifesto *On the Road*, 1951), Allen Ginsberg, and Lawrence Ferlinghetti among others. In 1955, Ginsberg read his incendiary poem *Howl*, which resulted in an infamous obscenity trial for his publisher, Lawrence Ferlinghetti; Kerouac memorialized the epic night in *Dharma Bums* (1958). The Merry Pranksters, led by Ken Kesey (*One Flew Over the Cuckoo's Nest*, 1962), and LSD-tinged exploits followed, described in Tom Wolfe's *The Electric Kool-Aid Acid Test*, 1968.

Armistead Maupin's 1976 *Tales of the City* chronicled the lives of young San Franciscans, and writers Maxine Hong Kingston (*The Woman Warrior*, 1975) and Amy Tan (*The Joy Luck Club*, 1989) wrote about the Chinese-American experience in San Francisco.

G

GAY TRAVELERS

San Francisco is internationally known as one of the world's most welcoming places for gays and lesbians, and this accepting attitude prevails in all neighborhoods. The most predominantly gay district is the Castro. The best source for information are two free weeklies: the *Bay Area Reporter* (www.ebar.com) and the *Bay Area Times* (www.sfbaytimes. com). Also consult www.onlyinsan francisco.com/gaytravel. The Center (1800 Market Street; tel: 865-5555; www.sfcenter.org; Mon–Fri noon–10pm, Sat 9am–10pm; free) is a vital nexus for the LGBT community, and has an information desk, library, web access, bulletin boards, and a café.

Above from far left: City Lights Bookstore, a magnet for book-worms; colorful gay pride mural in the Castro.

GUIDED TOURS

As well as the free (to guests of the Joie de Vivre hotel chain) Golden Gate Greeter tours, a range of free volunteer-led tours are offered by San Francisco City Guides (www.sfcityguides.org). Foot! (www.foottours.com), Wok Wiz Chinatown Tour (www.wokwiz.com), and Cruisin' the Castro (www.cruisin thecastro.com) also offer tours at reasonable prices.

HEALTH

Drugstores (Pharmacies)

Some medicines that are available over the counter in your home country may require a prescription in the U.S. Branches of the useful 24-hour Walgreens drugstore chain include:

498 Castro Street; tel: 861-3136; Metro: F, K, L, M, T to Castro.

1189 Potrero Avenue; tel: 647-1397; bus: 9, 33, 48.

3201 Divisadero Street; tel: 931-6417; bus: 28, 30, 43, 76.

Additional Walgreens and Rite Aid (www.riteaid.com) branches are open late into the evening.

Insurance and Hospitals

Healthcare is private and can be very expensive, especially if you need to be hospitalized. Foreign visitors should always ensure that they have full medical insurance covering their stay before traveling to the U.S. The following hospitals have 24-hour emergency rooms:

California Pacific Medical Center
Castro Street at Duboce Avenue; tel: 415-600-6000; www.cpmc.org; Metro: N to Duboce.

Saint Francis Memorial Hospital
900 Hyde Street; tel: 353-6300; www.saintfrancismemorial.org; bus: 1, 2, 19, 27, 31.

San Francisco General Hospital
1001 Potrero Avenue; tel: 206-8000; www.sfdph.org; bus: 9, 33, 48.

UCSF Medical Center
505 Parnassus Avenue; tel: 476-1000; www.ucsfhealth.org; Metro: N to UCSF.

INTERNET

Many cafés have Wi-Fi hotspots, and public library branches provide free web access (San Francisco Public Library; tel: 557-4400; http://sfpl.org). Internet cafés include:

Golden Gate Perk Internet Café
401 Bush Street; tel: 362-3929; Mon–Fri 8am–8pm, Sat 11am–6pm; Metro: F, J, K, L, M, N, T to Montgomery.

Quetzal Internet Café
1234 Polk Street; tel: 673-4181; www.coffeeandcocoa.com; Mon–Fri 6.30am–10pm, Sat–Sun 7.30am–10pm; bus: 1, 4, 19, 27, 31.

MEDIA

The largest regional newspaper is the *San Francisco Chronicle* (www.sfgate.com/chronicle); its Sunday "Pink Pages"

list art, music, and entertainment events. Free alternative weeklies are found in newspaper boxes, cafés, and bars. The four main weeklies are the *San Francisco Bay Guardian* (www.sfbg.com), *SF Weekly* (www.sfweekly.com), *San Francisco Bay Times* (www.sfbaytimes.com), and *Bay Area Reporter* (www.ebar.com). The last two are gay- and lesbian-oriented, and most easily found in the Castro. You can also consult online guides such as sfstation (www.sfstation.com), Flavorpill (http://sf.flavorpill.net), MetroWize (www.metrowize.com), and Nitevibe (www.nitevibe.com). The city's magazines include *San Francisco Magazine* (www.sanfran.com) and *7x7* (www.7x7sf.com).

MONEY

Currency

The dollar ($) is divided into 100 cents (¢). The coins are the penny (1¢), nickel (5¢), dime (10¢), quarter (25¢), and the less common half-dollar (50¢) and $1 coin. Common banknotes are the $1, $5, $10, $20, $50, and $100 bills.

Banks and Currency Exchange

Bank hours are generally Monday to Friday, from about 9am to 5pm. Some open on Saturday mornings. It's best to change foreign currency at airports, major banks downtown, or American Express offices.

ATMs

ATMs are at banks, some stores, and bars, and charge varying usage fees: check also with your bank at home.

Credit Cards

Credit cards are accepted at most restaurants, hotels, and stores.

Traveler's Checks

With the popularity of ATMs, credit cards, and debit cards, traveler's checks are increasingly less common. However, banks, stores, restaurants, and hotels generally accept traveler's checks in U.S. dollars. If yours are in foreign denominations, they must first be changed to dollars. Un-exchanged checks should be kept in your hotel safe. Record the checks' serial numbers in a separate place to facilitate refunds of lost or stolen checks.

P

POLICE

The emergency police number is 911 (no coins needed). The non-emergency number for the police is 553-0123.

POSTAL SERVICES

Post offices open at 8–9am and close at 5–6pm, Monday through Friday; the post office in the Macy's department store on Union Square (tel: 956-0131) is also open on Sunday. Use the Civic Center post office for general-delivery mail (poste restante).
U.S. Postal Service
Tel: 800-275-8777; www.usps.com.
Civic Center Post Office
101 Hyde Street; tel: 563-7284; Mon–Fri 9am–5pm; Metro: F, J, K, L, M, N, T to Civic Center.

Above from far left: pharmacy sign; police badge; taking advantage of Wi-Fi internet access at a local web café.

PUBLIC HOLIDAYS

National holidays are:
New Year's Day (Jan 1); Martin Luther King Jr. Day (3rd Mon in Jan); President's Day (3rd Mon in Feb); Memorial Day (Last Mon in May); Independence Day (July 4); Labor Day (1st Mon in Sept); Columbus Day (2nd Mon in Oct); Veterans Day (Nov 11); Thanksgiving Day (4th Thur in Nov); and Christmas (Dec 25).

S

SMOKING

Be careful where you light up in San Francisco: smoking laws are strict, and smoking is banned in many public places such as offices, shops, restaurants, and bars. Many hotels are completely non-smoking. The minimum legal age for smoking is 18 years old.

T

TAXES

In San Francisco, an 8.5 percent sales tax is added to the price of all goods and services; in surrounding cities, the sales tax is 8.25 percent. Hotels charge a 14 percent tax that generally will not be included in quoted rates.

TELEPHONES

Local calls are inexpensive; long-distance calls are decidedly not. Public phones accept coins and calling cards.

The San Francisco area code is 415, which you only need to dial from outside the city; the country code is 1. Toll-free numbers begin 1-800, 1-888, 1-877, or 1-866.

Directory enquiries: 411.

U.S. calls outside your area code: 1 + area code + phone number.

International calls: 011+ country code + phone number.

Operator: 0 for assistance with local calls; 00 for international calls.

TIME ZONES

San Francisco is on Pacific Standard Time. P.S.T. is three hours behind Eastern Standard Time (New York) and eight hours behind Greenwich Mean Time (London).

TIPPING

Tipping in the U.S. is different from many other places in the world. Most wait staff and bartenders make minimum wages only and depend on tips for survival. If you tip badly, don't expect great service if you return and you are recognized.

Restaurants: 15–20 percent (even if you were unsatisfied with the service you should tip 10 percent). Most restaurants add a service charge automatically for parties of six or more.

Taxis: 10–15 percent.

Bars: 10–15 percent, or at least $1–2 per drink.

Coat check: $1–2 per coat.

Door attendants: $1–2 for hailing a cab or bringing in bags.

Porters: $1–2 per bag (more if you packed bricks).

Valet parking: $2–3.

Concierge: $5–10.

Maids: $3–5 per day.

Hairdressers and salons: 15–20 percent.

TOURIST INFORMATION

Visitor Information Center of San Francisco

900 Market Street; tel: 391-2000; www.onlyinsanfrancisco.com; Nov–Apr Mon–Fri 9am–5pm, Sat 9am–3pm (May–Oct also Sun 9am–3pm); Metro: F, J, K, L, M, N, T to Powell; cable-car: Powell–Hyde, Powell–Mason. The center is down the stairway near the cable-car turntable at Market and Powell streets, and supplies brochures, maps, and helpful answers. Call for a listing of monthly events (in multiple languages).

TRANSPORTATION

A major hub for flights from all over the world, San Francisco is easily reached by air, while visitors from other parts of the United States can opt to travel by rail or bus. Once here, the city and its outlying areas are comfortably navigable by public transportation. In San Francisco, a car is not generally necessary to see the sights, and can prove to be something of a hassle, especially when such great views are provided on cable-cars from the tops of the city's hills. Efficient, affordable, and comprehensive, San Francisco's public transportation network makes it easy to be green.

Getting to San Francisco

By Air

San Francisco International Airport (SFO; 1 McDonnell Road; tel: 650-821-8211; www.flysfo.com) is the major international airport for northern California. From Europe, all the major airlines offer non-stop flights or connections via New York, Chicago, or Los Angeles. It also receives non-stop, or one-stop, flights from all the principal Pacific airports. For foreign travelers, many of the U.S. airlines offer deals for visiting several American cities.

Despite being 13 miles (21km) away, downtown San Francisco is easy to reach. Taxis and shuttles line the inner circle of the transportation zones of the Arrivals/Baggage Claim Level, while BART (Bay Area Rapid Transit), located at the Departures/Ticketing Level at the International Terminal and accessible from the Domestic Terminal by the Airtrain, takes passengers to downtown San Francisco and across the bay to various cities, for a minimal cost. The area is blanketed by Wi-Fi, which can be used for a fee.

The **Oakland International Airport** (OAK; 1 Airport Drive, Oakland; tel: 510-563-3300; www.flyoakland.com) is located 4 miles (6km) south of the city's downtown, and is accessible by BART. A hub for low-cost carriers, OAK is often a more economical alternative to the bigger and busier SFO.

The smallest of the three airports, **Mineta San Jose International Airport** (SJC; 1732 North 1st Street, San

Jose; tel: 408-501-7600; www.sjc.org) is nearly 50 miles (80km) from downtown San Francisco.

Carbon-Offsetting

Every day, airplanes dump 90 million lbs (41 million kg) of carbon dioxide and other noxious greenhouse gasses into the atmosphere. To "offset" their share of the carbon footprint, travelers can buy carbon credits according to the distance traveled. Credits invest money into renewable energy and energy efficiency programs. For more information visit www.sustainabletravelinternational.org or www.climatecare.org.

By Train

While **Amtrak** (Emeryville depot, 5885 Horton Street, Emeryville; tel: 510-450-1087 (information line: 800-872-7245; www.amtrak.com), the cross-continental passenger rail line, does not connect directly to San Francisco, it has a free shuttle to deliver passengers to and from the depot in Emeryville, located in the East Bay. For longer trips, Amtrak can be frustrating, as passenger trains share the rail lines with, and must defer to, the freight lines, causing significant delays. Nonetheless, it still remains a green alternative to air travel, and some routes are quite picturesque.

By Bus

Downtown, just east of Market Street, the **Transbay Terminal** (425 Mission Street; information line: 800-231-2222; www.greyhound.com; tel: 495-1555) is a major hub for the transcontinental **Greyhound** bus service.

The **Green Tortoise** (494 Broadway; information line: 800-8678-6473; www. greentortoise.com; tel: 956-7500) is a great alternative to Greyhound or even Amtrak. Each trip makes frequent stops at national parks or other points of interest, and their buses have communal areas that convert to reclined sleeping quarters at night. The San Francisco headquarters also house the Green Tortoise hostel.

By Car

Despite congestion, myriad hills, and the problem of what to do with your vehicle upon arriving, San Francisco is easy to reach by car. Interstates 101 and 80 pass through the city, while Interstates 5 and 99 are not too far away in the Central Valley. State Highway 1 runs along the coast of California and the western part of San Francisco.

Getting around San Francisco

For help navigating the entire Bay Area public transit system, including Muni buses and metro streetcars, and BART *(see below)*, call 511 or look online at www.511.org; 511 offers assistance with planning trips using public transportation, traffic, and drive time information, tips for traveling with bikes, and links to various municipal transit agencies.

BART (Bay Area Rapid Transit)

Fast, quiet, and efficient, BART (www.bart.gov) allows passengers to get around the Bay Area in comfort. All BART lines travel through San Francisco, extending to San Francisco International Airport, and under the

bay to Oakland, Berkeley, and beyond. Its stations provide maps that clearly explain routes and fares, and automatic ticketing machines from which passengers can purchase their tickets. If they do not have the exact change, passengers may carry a balance on their ticket for future use, or utilize one of the change machines also located in the stations.

Four BART lines run through downtown and provide the quickest way to travel between downtown and the Mission District, or to reach Oakland and Berkeley.

Buses and Metro

Muni, the San Francisco Municipal Transit Agency, runs the city's orange-and-white diesel and electric buses, streetcars which run on lightrail lines underground through downtown, the historic F-line streetcars (comprising a collection of vintage trams from all over the world), and of course, the cable-cars. "Muni" can be used to refer to the system as a whole and also to the Metro streetcars. The Muni Owl service replaces some lines between 1–5am.

Purchasing a map is highly recommended and will make a stay in San Francisco infinitely simpler. They cost $3 and are available at the Muni kiosks at the Powell and Market, and Powell and Beach cable-car terminals, as well as in some stores where general maps are sold. They are also posted at many Muni Metro and bus stops.

For all Muni Metro and bus lines, adult fare is $1.50. Exact change is necessary, but transfer slips are given, allowing you to transfer different Muni Metro or bus lines within a 90-minute timeframe. Ride without limit on Muni-operated transport, including the cable-cars, by using 1-, 3-, or 7-day visitor "Passports." They are sold at the baggage claim at San Francisco International Airport, on the mezzanine level of the Montgomery Muni Metro station, major cable-car terminals, and the kiosk at Bay and Taylor streets. For a list of other places where passes can be purchased, and for route planning and general information, see www.sfmta.com. For up-to-the-minute information on when the vehicle you are waiting for will arrive, refer to www.nextmuni.com.

Cable-Cars

Cable-cars are also operated by Muni, but are the exception to most of the Muni rules. Fares can be purchased at the kiosk at each terminal, or when you board. Drivers do give exact change, but no transfers. They are also considerably more expensive at $5 per trip. Often crowded with tourists, they ride over San Francisco's famous hills.

Taxis

Taxis are a convenient but expensive way to get about when the majority of San Francisco's public transit shuts down around 12:30am. They hover around popular tourist or nightlife spots, but in out-of-the-way locations it is advisable to call a radio-dispatched taxi.
DeSoto Cab Company, tel: 970-1300.
Green Cab, tel: 626-47336.
Luxor Cab Company, tel: 828-4141.
Yellow Cab, tel: 333-3333.

Above from far left: BART station in Berkeley; Embarcadero trams.

Riding the Cars
Taking a cable-car ride is one of the classic San Francisco experiences. However, waits to board at the cable-car turnaround at 5th and Market streets can be long. A better bet for speed and a seat may be to board the California line at Van Ness or the Ferry Building; the fine views on this route are of Nob Hill, Chinatown, and the Financial District.

Cycling

Around San Francisco, there are plenty of places to ride that are reasonably flat and far from exhaust fumes. Cycling through Golden Gate Park is a favorite, especially on Sundays, when many of the roads are vehicle-free. Riding along the Golden Gate Promenade and crossing the Golden Gate Bridge is a stunning ride, although difficult if the wind is up. Bikes can be rented hourly or for the day, with rates varying by type of bike, but usually $20–60 per day and $7–10 per hour.

Bay City Bike

2661 Taylor Street and 1325 Columbus Avenue; tel: 346-2453; www.baycity bike.com; daily from 8am; bus: 10, 30, 47.

Blazing Saddles

1095 Columbus Avenue, including a number of locations on Fisherman's Wharf; tel: 202-8888; www.blazing saddles.com; daily from 8am; Metro: F to Fisherman's Wharf.

Golden Gate Bike and Skate

3038 Fulton Street; tel: 668-1117; Mon–Tue 10am–6pm, Fri 10am–6pm, Sat–Sun 10am–7pm; bus: 5, 21, 31, 33.

Driving

San Francisco is a difficult city to drive and park in, often taxing the most experienced local drivers. It is crisscrossed by one-way streets, and the fast-paced driving culture can easily unnerve any visitor. If it is necessary to rent a car, all the major car-rental companies have outlets at San Francisco International Airport and around the city.

Avis Rental Car

821 Howard Street; tel: 957-9998; www.avis.com.

Enterprise

350 Beach Street; tel: 474-9600; www.enterprise.com.

Hertz Rent A Car

433 Mason Street; tel: 771-2200; www.hertz.com.

Walking

The best way to see San Francisco is by walking. Only 7 miles by 7 miles (127 sq. km), it is easy to cover great distances while seeing many different neighborhoods and glimpsing how residents live. Walking the hills provides spectacular views of the city and the rest of the Bay Area. Bring a map, comfortable shoes, and an extra layer of clothing in case the infamous San Francisco fog rolls in. Always be alert while crossing intersections. Taxis can be particularly aggressive.

Getting Around the Bay Area

Caltrain

Caltrain (main San Francisco depot, 700 4th Street; information line: 800-660-4287; www.caltrain.org) runs alongside Highway 101 to San Jose, with limited extensions all the way to Gilroy. It is largely a commuter train, but for visitors headed to the Peninsula or the South Bay, it is an enjoyable ride; there's plenty of comfortable seating, an upper deck with tables, and a car to accommodate passengers with bikes. Caltrain's terminus is near the AT&T Ballpark and many San Francisco Muni bus

and Metro lines, helpful for getting passengers around the city. Every Caltrain stop has an electronic ticket machine at which passengers can purchase tickets.

Ferries
Many locals use ferries for commuting, but for visitors, they can provide a great scenic and environmental alternative to driving. Departing from Fisherman's Wharf or the Ferry Building, they travel to Angel Island, and throughout the North and East Bay areas. Tickets can be purchased at the ticket windows next to the ferry terminals.
Blue and Gold Fleet, Pier 39 Marine Terminal, The Embarcadero at Beach Street; tel: 705-8200; www.blueand goldfleet.com.
Golden Gate Ferry, Ferry Building, The Embarcadero at Market Street; tel: 455-2000; www.goldengate ferry.org.

Intercity Buses
Neighboring transit systems also connect San Francisco with other Bay Area cities. These buses can be caught at various stops downtown, or at the Transbay Terminal, located at First and Mission streets.
Golden Gate Transit, Information line: 455-2000; www.goldengate.org.
Alameda Contra-Costa County Transit District, Information line: 510-891-4700; www.actransit.org.
San Mateo County Transit District Information line: 510-817-1717; www.samtrans.org.

V

VISA INFORMATION

U.S. citizens returning to the U.S. by air or land from Canada, Mexico, the Caribbean, and Bermuda will need a valid passport or other accepted identification. Under the current Visa Waiver Scheme, for nationals of 27 countries (including the U.K., Australia, and New Zealand) no visa is needed for stays in the U.S. of less than 90 days (for business or pleasure) upon showing an individual machine-readable passport. A return plane ticket is normally required. For passports renewed or extended between October 26, 2005, and October 25, 2006, a digital photograph printed on the data page or an integrated computer chip with information from the data page (known as an e-Passport) is required. Passports renewed on or after October 26, 2006, should automatically be e-Passports.

All other foreign citizens need visas. Application forms and information are available at U.S. embassies and consulates. Plan several weeks in advance as, depending on your country of residence and the time you wish to travel, the process can take a while. Be sure to double-check current requirements at http://travel.state.gov.

W

WEIGHTS AND MEASURES

The imperial system is standard.

There is no shortage of places to lay your hat in this city, with a dizzying array of hotels, motels, bed-and-breakfasts, and inns. Major chains are well represented, but more interesting rooms can often be found in boutique hotels: small, amenities-rich properties with a definable personality. When making reservations at the larger hotels, always ask about special packages and discounts, and check online booking agencies as rates are often better.

Fisherman's Wharf

Argonaut Hotel

495 Jefferson Street; tel: 563-0800; www.argonauthotel.com; Metro: F to Jones and Beach streets; cable-car: Powell–Hyde; $$$

Directly opposite the Wharf's Hyde Street Pier, the redbrick, maritime-themed Argonaut offers suites with spa tubs, telescopes, and sea views. Pet-friendly; non-smoking.

Tuscan Inn

425 North Point Street; tel: 561-1100; www.tuscaninn.com; Metro: F to Jefferson and Taylor streets; cable-car: Powell–Mason; $$

The Tuscan Inn is possibly the most pleasant of the many Fisherman's

---

Price per night for a standard double room, excluding taxes and breakfast unless noted.

$$$$	above 350 U.S. dollars
$$$	225–350 U.S. dollars
$$	150–225 U.S. dollars
$	below 150 U.S. dollars

Wharf hotels. Rooms are attractive and well sized by local standards, and families enjoy the proximity to Pier 39.

North Beach and Telegraph Hill

Hotel Boheme

444 Columbus Avenue; tel: 433-9111; www.hotelboheme.com; bus: 30, 39, 41, 45; $$

This small North Beach hotel has lovely little bedrooms graced with iron beds, brightly painted walls, and free Wi-Fi. Front-desk staff happily assist with hire cars, dinner reservations, and tours.

Washington Square Inn

1660 Stockton Street; tel: 981-4220; www.wsisf.com; bus: 30, 39, 41; $$

A European-style bed-and-breakfast that offers a great location for an extended exploration of North Beach's legendary dining and nightlife scenes.

Union Square and Financial District

Andrews Hotel

624 Post Street; tel: 563-6877; www.andrewshotel.com; bus: 2, 3, 27, 38, 76; $

Two blocks west of Union Square, this 1905 Victorian offers smallish rooms and baths and an included continental breakfast and evening wine reception. No smoking.

Campton Place Hotel

340 Stockton Street; tel: 781-5555; www.tajhotels.com; bus: 2, 4, 30, 45, 76; cable-car: Powell–Mason, Hyde–Mason; $$$$

Elegant, deluxe, and intimate, this most renowned and refined hotel offers excellent service, top-notch amenities, and a consistently highly rated restaurant.

Chancellor Hotel

433 Powell Street; tel: 362-2004; www.chancellorhotel.com; bus: 2, 3, 27, 38, 71; $$

Family-owned and managed since 1917, this charming, comfortably furnished hotel is a stone's throw from Union Square. Bathrooms are small but well stocked.

Clift Hotel

495 Geary Street; tel: 775-4700; www.clifthotel.com; bus: 2, 4, 27, 38, 76; $$$

Redesigned by Philippe Starck, this historic hotel is now a fusion of old-world elegance and contemporary style. It is also home to the Asia de Cuba restaurant and Redwood Room.

Four Seasons

757 Market Street; tel: 633-3000; www.fourseasons.com; Metro: F, J, K, L, M, N, T to Montgomery; cable-car: Powell–Hyde, Powell–Mason; $$$$

The Four Seasons boasts an ultra-convenient downtown location, an in-house tech-center, high-end stores, and a two-story health club with an indoor pool and Jacuzzi.

Handley Union Square Hotel

351 Geary Street; tel: 781-7800; www.handley.com/sf; bus: 2, 4, 27, 38, 71; $$

A good family choice, with a heated pool, Nintendo games, and morning and evening room service. Larger club rooms in an adjacent building offer fresh decor, dressing areas, and newspapers.

Hotel Monaco

501 Geary Street; tel: 292-0100; www.monaco-sf.com; bus: 2, 3, 27, 38, 76; $$

This renovated Beaux Arts building has hand-painted ceiling domes and grand Art Nouveau murals in common areas. Rooms are colorful, comfortable, and glamorous. Amenities include whirlpool tubs in most suites, yoga accessories, and 24-hour room service. Rates include coffee, afternoon tea, and wine-and-cheese receptions.

Hotel Nikko

222 Mason Street; tel: 394-1111; www.hotelnikkosf.com; Metro: F, J, K, L, M, N, T to Powell; cable-car: Powell–Mason, Powell–Hyde; $$$

The main draw at this elegant, sophisticated Japanese hotel is not so much the comfortable, well-equipped rooms as the spa facilities, which are among the city's best.

Hotel Rex

562 Sutter Street; tel: 433-4434; www.jdvhospitality.com; cable-car: Powell–Hyde, Powell–Mason; $

The sophisticated 1930s-styled Rex is dedicated to the literati, hosting book signings, poetry readings, and jazz on Fridays in the library bar. Complimentary evening wine hour and city tours are offered. Non-smoking.

Hotel Triton

342 Grant Street; tel: 394-0500; www.hoteltriton.com; bus: 2, 3, 30, 45, 76; $$

Across from Chinatown Gate, the eco-friendly Triton is a green hotel pioneer, employing a sophisticated recycling program, energy-efficient systems, and other environmentally conscious practices. The lobby's wild designs and mod furniture are amusing, though the bedrooms are tiny.

Mandarin Oriental

222 Sansome Street; tel: 800-622-0404; www.mandarinoriental.com; Metro: F, J, K, L, M, N, T to Montgomery; cable-car: California; $$$$

Enjoy jaw-dropping views and decadent service here. Binoculars are provided in each room; some have bathtubs near windows.

Ritz-Carlton

600 Stockton Street; tel: 296-7465; www.ritzcarlton.com; cable-car: California; $$$$

Once a giant neoclassical corporate headquarters, this luxury hotel now caters to giant pocketbooks with enormous rooms, a fitness center, indoor pool, and fine dining restaurant.

Price per night for a standard double room, excluding taxes and breakfast unless noted.

$$$$	above 350 U.S. dollars
$$$	225–350 U.S. dollars
$$	150–225 U.S. dollars
$	below 150 U.S. dollars

Serrano

405 Taylor Street; tel: 885-2500; www.serranohotel.com; bus: 27, 38; cable-car: Powell–Hyde, Powell–Mason; $$

A Spanish-Moroccan-styled hotel in the Theater District, with the tasty Ponzu restaurant downstairs. Kid- and pet-friendly.

Sir Francis Drake

450 Powell Street; tel: 392-7755; www.sirfrancisdrake.com; bus: 2, 3, 27, 38, 74; $$$

This 1928, recently renovated, landmark building offers smart, slightly clubby rooms, a small fitness room, nightclub, and spectacular views. The excellent Scala's Bistro is just next door.

Vantaggio Suites Cosmo

761 Post Street; tel: 673-6040; www.vantaggiosuites.com; bus: 2, 3, 4, 27, 76; $

Popular with an arty crowd thanks to art openings and a lobby filled with works by local artists, this suite hotel features facilities such as community kitchen and dining areas, fitness and recreation rooms. The corner suites with stunning views are a bargain.

Westin St Francis

335 Powell Street; tel: 397-7000; www.westinstfrancis.com; cable-car: Powell–Hyde, Powell–Mason; $$$

Legendary Union Square hotel with an on-site fitness center, room service and chef Michael Mina's acclaimed restaurant. If the historic aspects interest you, reserve a room in the original building: the baths here are

small and the rooms rather dark, but they are furnished with handsome reproductions and chandeliers.

York Hotel
940 Sutter Street; tel: 885-6800; www.yorkhotel.com; bus: 2, 3, 4, 27, 76; $

The setting for Hitchcock's *Vertigo* has recently been renovated and offers a deluxe continental breakfast with the very reasonable room rates. Here also is the Plush Room theater, once a Prohibition-era speakeasy, now known for torch singers and cabaret.

SoMa and Civic Center
Adagio Hotel
550 Geary Street; tel: 775-5000; www.thehoteladagio.com; bus: 27, 38; $$$

Comfortable and chic, with Aveda bath products, internet access, and superb customer service. Ask for a room with a view. Non-smoking.

Harbor Court Hotel
165 Steuart Street; tel: 882-1300; www.harborcourthotel.com; Metro: F to Don Chee Way and Steuart Street; $$$

Elegant boutique hotel in a 1907 building that offers comfortable rooms, luxury amenities, bay views, and complimentary access to the state-of-the-art fitness center next door.

Hotel Vitale
8 Mission Street; tel: 278-3700; www.hotelvitale.com; Metro: F, J, K, L, M, N, T to Embarcadero; $$$

A new addition to the waterfront with a slew of pampering amenities, such as complimentary yoga classes and free car service within 1 mile (1.6km).

InterContinental San Francisco
888 Howard Street; tel: 888-811-4273; www.intercontinentalsan francisco.com; bus: 14, 27; $$$

This towering green-glass hotel represents a brand-new benchmark in local luxury. Guest rooms have floor-to-ceiling windows and plenty of amenities.

Mosser
54 4th Street; tel: 986-4400; www.themosser.com; Metro: F, J, K, L, M, N, T to Powell; $$

An affordable choice for young sophisticates with good rates, location, and the latest gadgets. Still, the lobby's ornate stained glass, antique phone booths, and a sluggish elevator are quirky reminders of this hotel's past.

Palace Hotel
2 New Montgomery Street; tel: 512-1111; www.sfpalace.com; Metro: F, J, K, L, M, N, T to Montgomery; $$$$

This opulent historical landmark just south of Market is home to the magnificent Garden Court Restaurant. Enjoy cocktails under the Maxfield Parrish mural in the Pied Piper bar.

Phoenix Hotel
601 Eddy Street; tel: 776-1380; www.thephoenixhotel.com; bus: 19, 31; $

Funky rooms with bamboo furniture and a tropical oasis touch are found

Above from far left: smart uniform at the Westin St-Francis; entrance to the Hotel Vitale.

Book Ahead
Since San Francisco is a very popular convention and tourist town, it is imperative to make reservations well ahead of time. If you have not done so, phone SF Reservations, tel: 800-677-1500 (toll-free in U.S.) or 510-628-4400, or visit www.hotelres.com.

in this hotel that is popular with touring bands and edgy celebrities. The adjoining Bambuddah restaurant and bar also serves up Asian-themed delights poolside.

W Hotel

181 3rd Street; tel: 777-5300; www.whotels.com; bus: 9, 14, 30, 45, 76; $$$$

Sparse elegance and minimalist design are the allure of this swank hotel. The modernity extends to the well-stocked rooms, each with CD players, Wi-Fi, and goose-down duvets. The top-notch XYZ restaurant is downstairs.

Nob Hill

Fairmont Hotel and Tower

950 Mason Street; tel: 772-5013; www.fairmont.com; cable-car: California; $$$

The opulent and famous Fairmont on the crest of Nob Hill has been accommodating guests since 1907 (see p.59). Today, the spacious rooms and impeccable service attract a loyal clientele.

Huntington Hotel

1075 California Street; tel: 474-5400; www.huntingtonhotel.com; cable-car: California; $$$$

Price per night for a standard double room, excluding taxes and breakfast unless noted.

$$$$	above 350 U.S. dollars
$$$	225–350 U.S. dollars
$$	150–225 U.S. dollars
$	below 150 U.S. dollars

Across the street from Huntington Park atop Nob Hill, this classy, family-owned hotel built in 1924 attracts publicity-shy celebrities with discreet luxury, generously sized rooms, views (above the 8th floor), and one of the city's best spas.

InterContinental Mark Hopkins

1 Nob Hill; tel: 392-3434; www.ic hotelsgroup.com/intercontinental; cable-car: California; $$$

Situated where Mark Hopkins's mansion once stood, this hotel offers luxury rooms, grand views in all directions, and an atmosphere of quiet refinement. The rooftop cocktail lounge, Top of the Mark, has been a city staple since 1939.

Petite Auberge

863 Bush Street; tel: 928-6000; www.jdvhospitality.com; cable-car: Powell–Hyde, Powell–Mason; $

A small, cozy, French-style inn that offers a pretty parlor for afternoon wine and an included gourmet breakfast.

Renaissance Stanford Court

905 California Street; tel: 989-3500; www.mariott.com; cable-car: California; $$$

A fine renovation here set the standard for San Francisco grand hotel revivals. Enjoy great views and the quintessential San Francisco sound of cable-cars ding-dinging outside your window.

White Swan Inn

845 Bush Street; tel: 775-1755; www.jdvhospitality.com; cable-car: Powell–Hyde, Powell–Mason; $$

The romantic rooms and suites at this cozy, English-style bed-and-breakfast feature characterful fireplaces and comfortable sitting areas. Enjoy gourmet breakfast buffets, afternoon tea with home-baked cookies, and evening wine and hors d'oeuvres served fireside in the parlor.

Central Neighborhoods

Chateau Tivoli

1057 Steiner Street; tel: 776-5462; www.chateautivoli.com; bus: 21, 22; $

A plush Victorian bed-and-breakfast inn on picturesque Alamo Square brimming with antiques and curios. Some of the 22 attractive rooms feature fireplaces and Jacuzzis.

Hotel Del Sol

3100 Webster Street; tel: 921-5520; www.jdvhospitality.com; bus: 22, 43, 76; $

Once an ordinary motel, the Del Sol's radical makeover splashed color on walls, fabrics, and mosaic tiles decorating tabletops and walkways. Comfortable rooms surround a heated swimming pool, small lawn, and hammock; suites are available.

Hotel Majestic

1500 Sutter Street; tel: 441-1100; www.thehotelmajestic.com; bus: 2, 3, 4, 38; $$

An old-world atmosphere prevails at the Majestic, which was constructed in 1902 and claims to be the oldest still-operating hotel in the city. Rooms are cozy and festooned with swags and draperies. Good-value special rates.

Haight-Ashbury and Golden Gate Park

Inn 1890

1890 Page Street; tel: 386-0486; www.inn1890.com; bus: 7, 33, 37, 43, 71; $

This beautiful bed-and-breakfast built in 1890 is located just one block from Golden Gate Park. Some of the 18 rooms feature fireplaces.

Stanyan Park Hotel

750 Stanyan Street; tel: 751-1000; www.stanyanpark.com; bus: 7, 33, 43, 66, 71; $

Elegant and affordable, this early-20th-century boutique hotel is steps from Golden Gate Park and Haight Street. Suites are large and ideal for families; a continental breakfast is included.

The Mission and Castro

24 Henry Guesthouse

24 Henry Street; tel: 864-5686; www.24henry.com; Metro: K, L, M, T to Church; $

This late-1800s house in the Castro has been refurbished and turned into a guesthouse with a parlor and five bedrooms. The owners also have another Victorian guesthouse, Village House, just five blocks away.

Parker Guesthouse

520 Church Street; tel: 621-3222; www.parkerguestouse.com; Metro: J to Church Street and 18th Street; $

A relaxed and welcoming Castro guesthouse with 21 rooms (two with shared bathrooms), a garden, steam room, and terrycloth robes for every guest.

Above from far left: luxury hotel room; cozy lounge.

San Francisco is internationally known as a prime destination for foodies. From groundbreaking California and exciting fusion cuisines to adventurous ethnic dishes, the delicious and diverse options are guaranteed to please. With thousands of restaurants competing for your taste buds, those that don't make the grade soon fall from notice, and those that do are on everyone's lips. Some districts are known for particular fare, but nearly all neighborhoods offer an extensive menu of cuisines for every meal of the day.

Fisherman's Wharf

Albona

545 Francisco Street; tel: 441-1040; www.albonarestaurant.com; Tue–Sat D only; bus: 30, 39; $$$

An intimate and "homey" Istrian restaurant serving Northern Italian dishes influenced by the flavors of Central and Eastern Europe, such as pan-fried gnocchi in a cumin-spiced sirloin sauce, and braised rabbit with onions, honey, and juniper berries.

Ana Mandara

891 Beach Street, Ghirardelli Square; www.anamandara.com; tel: 771-8600; Mon–Fri L and D, Sat–Sun D

Price guide for a three-course meal and half a bottle of house wine for one person:

$$$$	above 100 U.S. dollars
$$$	50–100 U.S. dollars
$$	25–50 U.S. dollars
$	below 25 U.S. dollars

only; Metro: F to Jones and Beach streets; $$$

Upscale French-Vietnamese-inspired fare is served amidst exotic Far East decor. Delicious starters include crispy rolls with crab and shiitake mushrooms and striped bass ceviche.

McCormick and Kuleto's

900 North Point Street, Ghirardelli Square; tel: 929-1730; www.mccormickandschmicks.com; daily L and D; cable-car: Powell–Hyde; $$$

From the relaxed, redwood-paneled dining room, you can enjoy waterfront views of Alcatraz, Marin and historic ships as you choose from a huge variety of fresh, imaginative seafood dishes and American favorites.

Scoma's

Pier 47; tel: 771-4383; www.scomas.com; daily L and D; Metro: F to Jefferson and Taylor streets; $$$

For a glimpse of the working man's wharf, dine right on the pier at this old-school Italian spot that has served seafood, pasta, and its acclaimed clam chowder for over 40 years.

North Beach

Firenze by Night

1429 Stockton Street; tel: 392-8485; firenzebynight.ypguides.net; daily D; bus: 30, 41, 45; $$

The house specializes in traditional Northern Italian fare – pillowy-soft gnocchi, tender calamari, and pappardelle pasta Toscana with rabbit – but the long menu pleases all tastes. Try house-made limoncello with dessert.

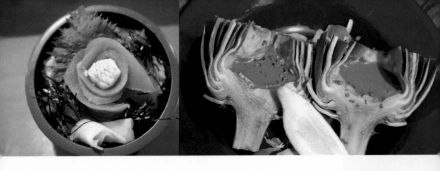

Helmand

430 Broadway; tel: 362-0641; www. helmandrestaurantsanfrancisco.com; Tue–Thur L and D, Fri–Mon D only; bus: 12, 30, 41, 83; $$

Afghan cuisine bursting with spice and flavor. Try the *bowlawni*: pastry shells stuffed with potato and leeks.

North Beach Restaurant

1512 Stockton Street; tel: 392-1700; www.northbeachrestaurant.com; daily L and D; bus: 30, 41, 45; $$$

A warm, relaxing spot featuring homemade pastas, home-cured prosciutto and other hearty Tuscan cuisine, plus a dizzyingly comprehensive wine list.

O'Reilly's

622 Green Street; tel: 989-6222; www.oreillysirish.com; daily B, L, and D; bus: 30, 41, 45; $

An Irish pub with hearty, generous portions: try the Guinness-battered fish and chips or the choice burgers.

Pena Pacha Mama

1630 Powell Street; tel: 646-0018; penapachamama.com; Wed–Sun D only; bus: 30, 41, 45; $$

Bolivian hospitality, robust organic flavors, traditional tapas like plantains and *yucca frita*, and live traditional music most nights make dining here an unforgettable experience.

Stella's Pastry and Café

466 Columbus Avenue; tel: 986-2194; daily B, L, and D; bus: 30, 41, 45; $

Cap a North Beach dinner with coffee and dessert at this beloved bakery. A good choice is the house specialty *sacripantina* (a divinely light and creamy layered cake laced with liquor) or mouthwatering *cannoli* and tiramisu.

Sushi on North Beach

745 Columbus Avenue; tel: 788-8050; www.northbeachsushi.com; Mon–Fri L and D, Sat–Sun D only; cable-car: Powell–Mason; $$$

Owner and chef Katsu provides a break from Italian-flavored North Beach with this tiny sushi spot. Expect unique rolls, fantastic miso soup, fine sake, and excellent vegetarian options.

Chinatown

Bix

56 Gold Street; tel: 433-6300; www.bixrestaurant.com; daily D; bus: 12, 41; $$$

Swank digs, upscale Californian munchies (from chef Bruce Hill, formerly of Aqua), and live jazz are served at this stylish, two-story supper club with plush banquettes and cozy booths.

Union Square, Financial District and Tenderloin

Aqua

252 California Street; tel: 956-9662; www.aqua-sf.com; Mon–Fri L and D, Sat–Sun D only; cable-car: California; $$$$

This sophisticated Californian seafood restaurant with two Michelin stars is consistently rated the city's best. World-class chefs work magic in the kitchen, and presentation and service are elegant and top-notch. Reservations required.

Above from far left: spicy ribs; beautiful presentation; San Francisco has many great Japanese restaurants; healthy artichoke dish.

Area Specialties
Some neighborhoods are known for a certain cuisine: burritos in the Mission; dim sum on Stockton and Broadway in Chinatown; Italian in North Beach; Indian and Vietnamese in the Tenderloin; and Chinese on the Inner Richmond's Clement Street.

Cortez

Hotel Adagio, 550 Geary Street; tel: 292-6360; www.cortezrestaurant.com; daily B and D only; bus: 27, 38; $$$

This celebrated fusion hotel restaurant holds its own against Union Square's best with exquisite, often organic, small plates of creative Mediterranean cuisine.

Fleur de Lys

777 Sutter Street; tel: 673-7779; www.fleurdelyssf.com; daily D; bus: 2, 3, 27, 76; $$$$

The city's premier French restaurant provides elegant and romantic formal fine dining, superior service, and an exhaustive wine list.

Kokkari

200 Jackson Street; tel: 981-0983; www.kokkari.com; Mon–Fri L and D, Sat D only; bus: 1, 12, 42, 83; $$$$

An upscale Greek taverna with beamed ceilings, massive fireplace, oriental carpets, and huge dishes of rich food. Reservations advisable.

Sam's Grill

374 Bush Street; tel: 421-0594; www.belden-place.com/samsgrill; Mon–Fri L and D; bus: 45, 76; $$$

Relive the days of three-Martini business lunches at this downtown grill, still going strong after 125 years. Dine on American cuisine in the high-ceilinged dining room or private booths.

Shalimar

532 Jones Street; tel: 928-0333; www.shalimarsf.com; daily L and D; bus: 27, 38; $

One of the city's best Indian restaurants, this simple spot serves Indian and Pakistani food in a noisy, relaxed atmosphere. No alcohol; cash only.

Slanted Door

1 Ferry Building #3; tel: 861-8032; www.slanteddoor.com; daily L and D; Metro: F to Embarcadero and Ferry Building; cable-car: California; $$$

Wholesome, flavorful, and modern Vietnamese food at one of the city's premier restaurants. At afternoon tea, sip hard-to-find Chinese varieties. Reservations required.

Tadich Grill

240 California Street; tel: 391-1849; Mon–Sat L and D; cable-car: California; $$$

Around in various incarnations since the Gold Rush, this institution offers old-school San Francisco ambience – from the original mahogany bar to the waiters as crusty as the sourdough – and a menu of classics including lobster Newburg, crab Louis, and sand dabs.

Taylor's Refresher

1 Ferry Building #6; tel: 866-328-3663; www.taylorsrefresher.com; daily L and D; Metro: F to the

---

Price guide for a three-course meal and half a bottle of house wine for one person:

$$$$	above 100 U.S. dollars
$$$	50–100 U.S. dollars
$$	25–50 U.S. dollars
$	below 25 U.S. dollars

Embarcadero and Ferry Building; cable-car: California; $

High-end diner fare with a gourmet flourish, from California beef burgers, to thick milkshakes and sweet-potato fries.

South of Market

Le Charm

315 5th Street; tel: 546-6128; www.lecharm.com; Tue–Fri L and D, Sat–Sun D only; bus: 12, 27, 30, 45; $$

Ratatouille, *escargots*, duck confit, crème brûlée, French onion soup: French food's greatest hits share this comfortable, unpretentious stage.

Town Hall

342 Howard Street; tel: 908-3900; www.townhallsf.com; Mon–Fri L, Sat–Sun L and D; bus: 12, 30, 45, 76; $$$

Regional American classics such as shrimp étouffée, buttermilk fried chicken, and Chimay-braised short ribs are served in a stylishly remodeled historic building.

Yank Sing

49 Stevenson Street; tel: 541-4949; www.yanksing.com; Mon–Fri 11am–3pm, Sat–Sun 10am–4pm; Metro: F, J, K, L, M, N, T to Montgomery; $$

A sure-fire dim sum pleaser, with fresh ingredients in a sparkling clean interior and particularly tasty dumplings.

Civic Center and Hayes Valley

Ananda Fuara

1298 Market Street; tel: 621-1994; www.anandafuara.com; Mon–Tue & Thur–Sat B, L and D, Wed B and L only; Metro: F, J, K, L, M, N, T to Civic Center; $

This is a sure bet for inexpensive, delicious, and varied vegetarian picks, from curry wraps to mushroom ravioli and vegan chocolate cake.

Espetus

1686 Market Street; tel: 552-8792; www.espetus.com; daily L and D; Metro: F, J, K, L, M to Van Ness; $$$ (prix fixe)

Eat until you burst at this Brazilian steakhouse in the South American *Churrascaría* style. Copious skewered meats are brought to your table and carved on the spot.

Zuni Café

1658 Market Street; tel: 552-2522; www.zunicafe.com; Tue–Sun L and D; Metro: F, J, K, L, M, N, T to Van Ness; $$

Zuni offers a California cuisine-based menu that never makes a mistake, from the roasted chicken and bread salad (for two) to the burger with shoestring potatoes that has a cult following. Reservations recommended.

Nob Hill and Russian Hill

1550 Hyde Café and Wine Bar

1550 Hyde Street; tel: 775-1550; www.1550hyde.com; Tue–Sun D only; cable-car: Powell–Hyde; $$$

Right on the cable-car route, this casually elegant neighborhood gem offers delectable seasonal and organic Californian offerings and an excellent wine selection.

Above from far left: gourmet scallops; racks of wine; super-fresh mussels; top marks for presentation.

Parking

Parking charges in San Francisco, especially downtown, can be crippling. If you do not want to pay the exorbitant lot rates, arrive at least 20 minutes early to find street parking, more likely in North Beach. Remember, always read street signs and curbs for parking restrictions.

Big 4

1075 California Street; tel: 771-1140; www.huntingtonhotel.com; Mon–Fri B, L, and D, Sat–Sun Br, L, and D; cable-car: California; $$$

Dark wood and railroad tycoon memorabilia add to this American restaurant's men's-club ambience, which has a menu that is heavy on meat and game.

Little Thai

2065 Polk Street; tel: 771-5544; Sun–Mon D only, Tue–Sat L and D; bus: 12, 19, 27, 47, 49; $

A great pick from the collection of Polk Gulch's Thai restaurants, Little Thai offers dependably delicious dishes like Pad See Ew and pumpkin curry.

Zarzuela

2000 Hyde Street; tel: 346-0800; Mon–Sat L and D; cable-car: Powell–Hyde; $$

Bring hungry friends to this cheerfully sophisticated Spanish restaurant atop Russian Hill and share tapas, paella, and sangria as cable-cars roll by.

Central Neighborhoods
Kiss

1700 Laguna Street; 474-2866; Tue–Sat D only; bus: 2, 3, 38; $$$

This bite-sized spot is perhaps the city's best Japanese restaurant, with outstanding sushi and sake, a simple and elegant atmosphere, and great service.

NOPA

560 Divisadero Street; tel: 864-8643; www.nopasf.com; daily D only; bus: 21, 24; $$$

Eclectic, wood-fired cuisine is the specialty here, from pork chops with grilled peaches to spicy fennel sausage flatbreads and tasty fried fish. Open until 1am.

Pres a Vi

1 Letterman Drive, Building D Suite 150; tel: 409-3000; www.presavi.com; Mon L, Tue–Fri L and D, Sat–Sun Br, L, and D; bus: 41, 43, 45; $$$

Think stellar fusion cuisine served up in the George Lucas compound in the Presidio. The unique location is no crutch for scrumptious small-plate seafood and savory specials.

Haight-Ashbury and Golden Gate Park
Arizmendi Bakery

1331 9th Avenue; tel: 566-3117; www.arizmendibakery.org; Tue–Fri 7am–7pm, Sat 8am–7pm, Sun 8am–4pm; Metro: N to Judah Street and 9th Avenue; $

On the Inner Sunset's main drag, this worker-owned co-operative sells fresh bread, pastries, artisan shortbread, and a special daily pizza with a sourdough crust.

The Mission and Castro
Bissap Baobab

2323 Mission Street; tel: 826-9287; www.bissapbaobab.com; Tue–Sun D only; bus: 14, 33, 49; $$

A funky international spot with a diverse clientele, serving West African fare and refreshing, potent cocktails. Standout dishes include spinach pastelle

pastry, *mafe* with tofu in a peanut sauce, and oniony chicken *dibi* with couscous.

Café Gratitude

2400 Harrison Street; tel: 824-4652; www.cafegratitude.com; daily B, L, and D; bus: 27, 41; $$

This off-the-beaten-path gem boasts an easygoing atmosphere, friendly staff, and vegan, vegetarian, and raw food including soups, salads, pizzas, and smoothies.

Conduit

280 Valencia Street; tel: 552-5200; www.conduitrestaurant.com; Tue–Sun D only; BART: 16th Street; $$$

The sleek, industrialist decor draws wows (the bar and ceiling are lined with steel- and copper-coated pipes) and so does the food. Try dishes such as spare ribs, halibut with roasted artichoke, or game hen with green-pea ravioli.

Panchita's

3115 22nd Street; tel: 821-6660; www.panchitas3.net; Tue–Sun D only; bus: 12, 14, 49; $$

A mix of California and Salvadorian semi-fine dining, great for small groups or romantics who like to venture off the beaten path.

Price guide for a three-course meal and half a bottle of house wine for one person:

$$$$	above 100 U.S. dollars
$$$	50–100 U.S. dollars
$$	25–50 U.S. dollars
$	below 25 U.S. dollars

Puerto Alegre

546 Valencia Street; tel: 255-8201; daily L and D; BART: 16th Street; $

Boisterous groups descend on this Mexican table-service restaurant to get well fed and a little tipsy from pitchers of Margaritas.

Range

842 Valencia Street; tel: 282-8283; www.rangesf.com; daily D only; BART: 24th Street; $$

This warm, inviting space serves savory contemporary Californian cuisine (scoring a Michelin star); the short but excellent menu includes dishes such as roasted chicken with an artichoke, toasted almond, and bacon bread salad.

Outer Neighborhoods

Aziza

5800 Geary Boulevard; tel: 752-2222; www.aziza-sf.com; daily D; bus: 38; $$$

Hike to the Outer Richmond and be rewarded with upscale, modern versions of Moroccan dishes. The menu is influenced by California cuisine's emphasis on organic, locally produced ingredients.

Sutro's at the Cliff House

1090 Point Lobos; tel: 386-3330; www.cliffhouse.com; daily L and D; Metro: N to Ocean Beach; $$$

Incredible views of the ocean, Golden Gate, and Marin Headlands make this smart, well-designed Ocean Beach restaurant a truly desirable option for seasonal California cuisine.

Above from far left: hot-dog sign; some of the excellent Californian grapes; colorful, fresh peppers; pretty dessert.

Tipping

Tipping in the U.S. is not optional: tipping 10 percent means that you were unsatisfied with the service; 15 percent is standard, but not great; and 20 percent means you were happy with both service and food. Percentages are calculated pre-tax. A quick way of calculating is to double the tax (8.5 percent) and round up or down depending on level of satisfaction.

San Francisco provides an enticing array of cultural diversions. Operatic arias and symphonic melodies waft through concert halls, jazz bands sizzle in intimate clubs, and hot rock, pop, and alternative bands jam on small stages and in spacious arenas alike. Theatrical flavors and fancy footwork run the gamut from classical to cutting-edge, and cinephiles enjoy much-loved art-house theaters and film festivals. The thirsty and hard-partying sets are not disappointed either, with sounds and spirits for all tastes.

Bars and Clubs

Amelie

1754 Polk Street; tel: 292-6916; www.ameliesf.com; daily 6pm–2am; bus: 1, 12, 19, 27

This sultry, crimson-walled wine bar features a French-heavy menu, classy clientele, and inviting atmosphere.

Bourbon and Branch

501 Jones Street; tel: 346-1735; www.bourbonandbranch.com; daily 5pm–3am; bus: 2, 3, 27, 76

A speakeasy without sidewalk signage where masterfully mixed libations are poured. Passwords "books" or "cigar" get you into the "Library" and "Russell's Room"; reserve to access the main bar.

Cav Wine Bar

1666 Market Street; tel: 437-1770; www.cavwinebar.com; Mon–Sat 5:30–11pm (Fri–Sat until midnight); Metro: F, J, K, L, M, N, T to Van Ness

Sidle up alongside professionals and connoisseurs at the sleek zinc bar and peruse a 300-plus wine list.

Edinburgh Castle

950 Geary Street; tel: 885-4074; www.castlenews.com; daily 5pm–2am; bus: 2, 3, 19

This Scottish-run Tenderloin pub offers quiz nights, poetry readings, local bands, pool and darts, a fantastic Scotch inventory, plus fish and chips.

El Rio

3158 Mission Street; tel: 282-3325; www.elriosf.com; Mon–Thur 5pm–2am, Fri–Sun 1pm–2am; BART: 24th Street

Diverse crowds flock to this friendly, funky bar for popular "Salsa Sundays" on the patio.

The End Up

401 6th Street; tel: 646-0999; www.theendup.com; Thur 10pm–4am, Fri 11pm–Sat 1pm, Sat 10pm–Mon 4am; bus: 12, 19, 27, 47

A diverse, gay-friendly crowd dances and carouses until dawn and beyond in this South of Market club.

Hemlock Tavern

1131 Polk Street; tel: 923-0923; www.hemlocktavern.com; daily 4pm–2am; bus: 1, 2, 19, 47, 49

Underground rock bands light up the back; hipster punk rockers snack on warm peanuts up front. Bonus: heated outdoor smoking lounge.

Matrix Fillmore

3138 Fillmore Street; tel: 563-4180; www.matrixfillmore.com; Mon–Thur 8pm–2am, Fri–Sun 6pm–2am; bus: 22, 45

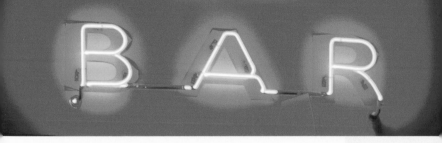

A fixture of the young Marina singles scene that is awash with designer jean-clad beauties.

Mezzanine

444 Jessie Street; tel: 625-8880; www.mezzaninesf.com; hours vary; BART: to Powell; Metro: F, J, K, L, M, N, T to Powell; bus: 6, 7, 14, 21, 26

Dance to beats from international and hot new talents at this mega-club located in South of Market.

Noc Noc

557 Haight Street; tel: 861-5811; www.nocnocs.com; daily 5pm–2am; bus: 6, 7, 22, 66

An easygoing, fun-loving crowd fills this funky Lower Haight dive with Flintstones c.1986 decor.

Ruby Skye

420 Mason Street; tel: 693-0777; www.rubyskye.com; Thur–Sat 8pm–4am; Metro: F, J, K, L, M, N, T to Powell

Major DJs pack this massive Union Square club with dancing crowds.

Top of the Mark

1 Nob Hill; tel: 616-6916; www.topofthemark.com; Mon–Sat 6:30am–2:30am, Sun 10am–midnight; cable-car: California

Sip cocktails looking down on the city from this elegant bar on "Snob Hill."

Zeitgeist

199 Valencia Street; tel: 255-7505; daily 9am–2am; Metro: K, L, M, T to Church

Tattooed hipsters soak up sun on the large, bench-filled patio, consuming burgers, brews, and Bloody Marys.

Cabaret

Asia SF

201 9th Street; tel: 255-2742; www.asiasf.com; Tue–Sun D only; Metro: F, J, K, L, M, N, T to Civic Center

"Gender illusionists" serve Cal-Asian cuisine and saucy entertainment every hour on the red runway bar.

Beach Blanket Babylon

Club Fugazi, 678 Green Street; tel: 421-4222; www.beachblanketbabylon.com; Wed–Thur 8pm, Fri–Sat 6:30pm and 9:30pm, Sun 2pm and 5pm; bus: 12, 15, 30, 45

A campy pop-culture spoof and legendary experience. Adults only except for Sunday matinees. Arrive early.

Teatro ZinZanni

Pier 29; tel: 438-2668; love.zinzanni.org; Wed–Sat 6:55pm, Sun 5:55pm (Dec: also Tue 6:55pm); Metro: F to Embarcadero and Sansome streets

Over-the-top cabaret, circus, and spectacle are served during an eclectic five-course dinner. Arrive early.

Classical Music

Louise M. Davies Symphony Hall

201 Van Ness Avenue; tel: 864-6000; www.sfsymphony.org; Metro: F, J, K, L, M, N, T to Van Ness

This elegant hall houses the acclaimed San Francisco Symphony Orchestra from September to July.

Above from far left: spoilt for choice at the Redwood Room, the hip watering hole at the Clift Hotel (see p.109); bright lights of the bar.

Tickets

TIX Bay Area (tel: 433-7827; www.tixbayarea.com) in Union Square sells half-price performance-day tickets from 11am. Other third-party ticket agents (which will add a booking fee) include Tickco.com (tel: 800-279-4444; www.tickco.com) and City Box Office (tel: 392-4400; www.cityboxoffice.com).

War Memorial Opera House

301 Van Ness Avenue; tel: 864-3330; www.sfopera.com; Metro: F, J, K, L, M, N, T to Van Ness

The glamorous Beaux Arts War Memorial Opera House fills from September to November and May to July with those keen to hear the San Francisco Opera Company perform.

Other Venues

Outside the two main venues above, the city's major companies perform at the Yerba Buena Center for the Arts (YBCA; *see p.50*) and the Herbst Theater in the War Memorial Veterans Building *(see p.56)*. Old First Presbyterian Church (1751 Sacramento Street; tel: 474-1608; www.oldfirstconcerts.org; bus: 1, 19, 47, 49; cable-car: California) runs a chamber and recital repertoire.

Comedy

North Beach houses the city's major comedy clubs. These include: **Cobb's Comedy Club** (915 Columbus Avenue; tel: 928-4320; www.cobbscomedyclub. com), **The Punchline** (444 Battery Street; tel: 397-7573; www.punchline comedyclub.com), and **Purple Onion** (140 Columbus Avenue; tel: 956-1653; www.purpleonioncomedy.com).

Contemporary Music

Bimbo's 365 Club

1025 Columbus Avenue; tel: 474-0365; www.bimbos365club.com; cable-car: Powell-Mason

Rock, jazz, and more swing this swank 1930s-throwback nightclub, which also has comedy and burlesque on occasion.

Fillmore Auditorium

1805 Geary Boulevard; tel: 346-6000; www.thefillmore.com; bus: 2, 3, 22, 38

Major headliners play this legendary venue where Bill Graham launched his empire in the 1960s.

Great American Music Hall

859 O'Farrell Street; tel: 885-0750; www.musichallsf.com; bus: 2, 3, 27, 38

A former Barbary Coast bordello complete with ornate balconies now attracts international rock, folk, and blues acts.

The Independent

628 Divisadero Street; tel: 771-1421; www.theindependentsf.com; bus: 21, 24

Popular for live rock, punk, indie pop, folk, hip-hop, and more.

Slim's

333 11th Street; tel: 255-0333; www.slims-sf.com; bus: 12, 19, 47

Packed SoMa spot with a mix of blues, R&B, and alternative touring acts.

Dance

The San Francisco Ballet (tel: 865-2000; www.sfballet.org) performs traditional full-length ballets and contemporary pieces from February through April at the War Memorial Opera House *(see above)*, and an ever-popular winter *Nutcracker* production. Alonzo King's LINES Ballet (tel: 863-3040; www.linesballet.org) is a top-notch globetrotting contemporary ballet company that performs locally at the YBCA *(see p.50)*. Another contem-

porary company is ODC Dance (tel: 863-6606; www.odcdance.org), known nationally for its artistic innovation.

369-6201; www.amctheatres.com) with its Imax and 15 theaters, San Francisco boasts unique art-house theaters, including the beloved Clay Theatre *(see p. 65)*, Red Vic *(see p. 75)*, Castro Theatre *(see p. 77)*, and The Roxie *(see p. 80)*.

Jazz and Blues

Biscuits and Blues

401 Mason Street; tel: 292-2583; www.biscuitsandblues.com; Tue–Thur 8–11:30pm, Fri–Sat 3:30–11:30pm; Metro: F, J, K, L, M, N, T to Powell; cable-car: Powell–Hyde, Powell–Mason

A nationally well-respected blues club that teams Southern cuisine with live blues and a relaxed atmosphere.

Boom Boom Room

1601 Fillmore Street; tel: 673-8000; www.boomboomblues.com; Tue–Sat 8pm; bus: 22, 38

Blues, boogie, groove, and soul keep this funky little joint hopping.

Jazz at Pearl's

256 Columbus Avenue; tel: 291-8255; www.jazzatpearls.com; daily 8pm and 10pm; bus: 20, 30, 41, 45

The intimate, plush ambience of a 1930s-style speakeasy is the backdrop for ace jazz acts.

Yoshi's

1330 Fillmore Street; tel: 655-5600; www.yoshis.com; shows: Mon–Sat 8pm and 10pm, Sun 7pm and 9pm, restaurant: daily D only; bus: 22, 31

Jazz giants jam at this outpost of Oakland's famed Jack London Square club.

Movies

In addition to the AMC Theaters at the Metreon (101 4th Street; tel:

Theater

American Conservatory Theater

415 Geary Street; tel: 749-2228; www.act-sf.org; cable-car: Powell–Hyde, Powell–Mason

A Tony Award-winning regional theater that delivers solid classical and contemporary fare.

Curran Theater

445 Geary Street; tel: 551-2000; www.shnsf.com; Metro: F, J, K, L, M, N, T to Powell; cable-car: Powell–Hyde, Powell–Mason

Broadway favorites and tryouts are staged in this elegant, historic theater.

Magic Theatre

Fort Mason Center, Building D, at Marina Boulevard and Buchannan Street; tel: 441-8822; www.magic theatre.org; bus: 10, 22, 28, 30, 47, 49

Dedicated to new works, this stage has premièred an impressive list of plays.

Orpheum Theatre

1192 Market Street; tel: 551-2000; www.shnsf.com; Metro: F, J, K, L, M, N, T to Powell; cable-car: Powell–Hyde, Powell–Mason

Large-scale Broadway productions fill this grand, historical landmark.

Above from far left: San Francisco has world-class venues for classical music; the Castro has a great LGBT-friendly scene; celebrations at the bar; Maya Lawson performing in *The K of D* at the Magic Theatre.

Fringe Theaters
The city's fringe theater venues include: Exit Theatre (tel: 673-3847; www.sffringe.org), Intersection for the Arts (tel: 626-2787; www.theintersection. org), The Marsh (tel: 800-838-3006; www.themarsh.org), the New Conservatory Theatre Center (tel: 861-8972; www.nctcsf. org), and Project Artaud Theatre (tel: 626-4370; www.artaud.org).

CREDITS

Insight Step by Step San Francisco
Written by: Barbara Rockwell and Anne Cherian
Series Editor: Clare Peel
Cartography Editors: Zoë Goodwin and James Macdonald
Picture Manager: Steven Lawrence
Art Editor: Ian Spick
Production: Kenneth Chan

Photography: All pics APA Team Nowitz except 4corners 11B; Alamy 20–1, 23; Corbis 62B, 23B; iStockphoto 12TL, 13TL, 35B, 35T, 8890TL, 90/91, 112TL; Photolibrary 8/9.
Front cover: main image: getty; bottom left: Britta Jaschinski; bottom right: Team Nowitz.

Printed by: CTPS-China.

First Edition 2009
Reprinted 2011

DISTRIBUTION

Worldwide
APA Publications GmbH & Co. Verlag KG (Singapore branch)
7030 Ang Mo Kio Ave 5
08-65 Northstar @ AMK, Singapore 569880
Email: apasin@singnet.com.sg

UK and Ireland
GeoCenter International Ltd
Meridian House, Churchill Way West
Basingstoke, Hampshire RG21 6YR
Email: sales@geocenter.co.uk

US
Ingram Publisher Services
One Ingram Blvd, PO Box 3006
La Vergne, TN 37086-1986
Email: customer.service@ingrampublisher services.com

Australia
Universal Publishers
PO Box 307
St. Leonards NSW 1590
Email: sales@universalpublishers.com.au

New Zealand
Hema Maps New Zealand Ltd (HNZ)
Unit 2
10 Cryers Road
East Tamaki
Auckland 2013
Email: sales.hema@clear.net.nz

CONTACTING THE EDITORS

We would appreciate it if readers would alert us to errors or outdated information by writing to us at insight@apaguide.co.uk or APA Publications, PO Box 7910, London SE1 1WE, UK.

www.insightguides.com

THE WORLD OF
INSIGHT GUIDES

Different people need different kinds of travel information.
Some want background facts. Others seek personal
recommendations. With a variety of different products – Insight
Guides, Insight City Guides, Step by Step Guides, Smart Guides,
Insight Fleximaps and our new Great Breaks series –
we offer readers the perfect choice.

Insight Guides will turn your visit into an experience.

www.insightguides.com

INDEX

A

age restrictions **96**
airports **103–4**
Alamo Square **8–9, 11**
Alcatraz **10, 11, 22, 28, 33–5, 84**
Alta Plaza Park **65, 66**
American Zoetrope Studios **37**
Amoeba Music **75**
Anchorage Hotel **30**
Angel Island **24**
Aquarium of the Bay **28**
Aquatic Park **31**
Argonaut Hotel **31**
Asian Art Museum **13, 54, 55**

B

Balmy Alley **83**
Bank of America **23**
bars **21, 120–1**
Beat generation **10, 23, 25, 36, 38, 68**
Beat Museum **38**
Berkeley **90–3**
  Berkeley Art Museum and
    Pacific Film Archive **93**
  Botanical Gardens **91–2**
  Doe Library **90–1**
  Hearst Museum of
    Anthropology **92–3**
  Lawrence Hall of Science
    91–2
  Moffitt Library **90**
  Memorial Glade **91**
  People's Park **93**
  Sather Gate **93**
  Sather Tower **91**
  Sproul Plaza **93**
  Telegraph Avenue **93**
  University of California **90–3**
  Valley Life Sciences Building
    90
Brocklebank Building **59–60**
Buena Vista Park **76–7**
Bullitt **22**

C

cabaret **121**
Cable-Car Museum **61**
cable-cars **10, 11, 24, 31, 52, 60, 61, 63, 105**
Caen, Herb **25**
Caffe Trieste **38**
California Historical Society **48**
Cannery, the **31**
Capone, Al **34**
cars and driving **104, 106**
Cartoon Art Museum **47**
Castro **11, 19, 76–8**
Castro Theater **77–8, 123**
Chestnut Street **86**
children **96**
Chinatown **10, 11, 16, 19, 24, 41–6**
Chinatown Gate **41, 42, 46**
Chinese Culture Center **44**
Chinese Historical Society of
  America **46**
Chinese New Year **44**
Chinese Telephone Exchange **41**
City Hall **55–6**
City Lights Bookstore **22, 37–8**
Civic Center **53–6**
Clay Theater **65, 123**
Cliff's Variety **78**
climate **12, 96**
clothing **16, 96**
clubs **21, 120–1**
Coit Tower **24, 36, 40**
Columbus Avenue **37**
comedy clubs **122**
Condor Club **38**
Constellation **53**
Contemporary Jewish
  Museum **50**
Coppola, Francis Ford
  22, 37, 38
Cow Hollow **11, 19**
crime and safety **96–7**
Crissy Field **87–8**
customs **97**

D

dance **57, 122–3**
de Young Museum **13, 25, 70–1**
Different Lights Bookstore **78**
disabled travelers **97**
Donaldina Cameron House **46**
dot-com era **10, 25**
Dragon House **43**
drink **17**
drugstores (pharmacies) **100**
Duke Ellington **20, 25**

E

earthquakes **10, 12, 24, 25, 37**
electricity **97**
Embarcadero **16, 19**
embassies and consulates **97**
emergency numbers **97**
entertainment **20–1**
  listings **120–3**
environment **13**
etiquette **16**
Exploratorium **85–6**

F

1907 Firehouse **61–2**
Fairmont San Francisco hotel
  58, 59
fashion **18, 82**
Fay Park **63**
Ferlinghetti, Lawrence **10**
ferries **107**
Ferry Building **19**
festivals **20, 21, 44, 97**
Feusier House **61**
Filbert Steps **40**
Fillmore **19, 20, 64–5, 67**
Financial District **15, 16, 18–19**
Fish Alley **30**
Fisherman's Wharf **16, 28–32**
Fishermen and Seamen's
  Chapel **31**
Fitzgerald, Ella **20, 25**

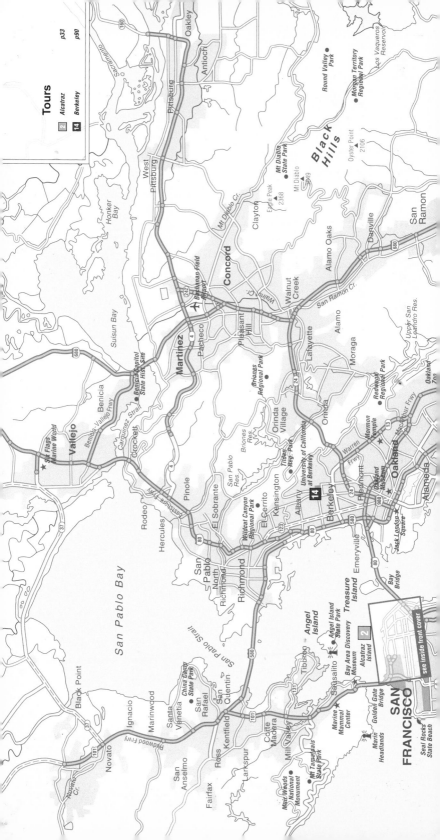

P

Pacific Bell Park stadium 25
Pacific Heights 11, 19, 64–9
Pacific Union Club 59
Palace of the Arts 86
Palace of Legion of Honor 11
Panama-Pacific Exposition 24
Parker, Charley 20, 25
Pelosi, Nancy 25
people 12, 82, 83
Pier 39 28
Pier 45 30
Pink Triangle Park and
    Memorial 77
police 101
Polk Street 16, 63
Portsmouth Square 44
postal services 101
Powell-Hyde cable-car 31, 32
Precita Eyes Mural Arts and
    Visitor Center 83
Presidio, the 84, 88
Presidio Heights 19
public holidays 102

R

recommended tours 6–7
Red Vic Movie House 75, 123
Richmond 11
Ripley's Believe It or Not! 29
Rivera, Diego 40
Roxie, the 80–1, 123
Russian Hill 11, 19, 36, 58–63

S

St Mary's Square 43
Sts Peter and Paul Church 22, 39
San Francisco Art Institute
    62–3
San Francisco Carousel 28
San Francisco Fringe Festival 21
San Francisco Museum of
    Modern Art 13, 48, 49
San Francisco National
    Maritime Museum 31

San Francisco Public Library,
    Main Branch 53–4
sea lions 28, 29
Sentinel Building 37
SFMOMA Artists Gallery 84
shopping 18–19, 43–4, 51, 52,
    57, 65, 75, 78, 82
Slims 20
smoking 102
Society of California
    Pioneers Museum 50
Society of the Sacred Heart 67
South of Market (SoMA) 13,
    16, 21, 47–52
spas 58, 59, 64
sport 87
Spreckels Mansion (Castro) 76
Spreckels Mansion (Pacific
    Heights) 65–6
S.S. Jeremiah O'Brien 30
Stein, Gertrude 14
Stockton Street 45
"Summer of Love" 10, 25, 74
Sun Yat-sen, Dr. (statue) 43
Sunset (district) 11

T

taxis 105
Telegraph Hill 36, 40
telephones 102
Tenderloin 16, 19
theater 21, 77–8
Tin Hou Temple 46
time zones 102
tipping 102
Toklas, Alice B. 14
tourist information 103
Transamerica Pyramid 23, 25
Transbay Terminal 25
transportation 103–7
Treaty of Guadalupe Hildago 24
Twin Peaks 77

U

Union Square 18, 21, 52
Union Street 68

United Commercial Bank 45
University of California,
    Berkeley 90–3 (see Berkeley)
U.S.S. Pampanito 30

V

Valencia Street 82
Vertigo 22, 23
Vesuvio Café 38, 40
Victorian Park 31
visas 107

W

War Memorial Opera House 10,
    25, 56–7, 122
War Memorial Veterans
    Building 56
Warfield Theater 20
Washington Square 22–3
Washington Square Park 39
Waters, Alice 14
Wave Organ 85
Waverly Place 46
Wax Museum 29
Wedding House 68
weights and measures 107
Westfield San Francisco
    Shopping Center 52
Whalen, Philip 10
Whittier Mansion 66, 67
Women's Building 81

X

Xanadu Gallery 52

Y

Yerba Buena 24, 44, 49
Yerba Buena Gardens 49
Yerba Buena Center for
    the Arts 50

Z

Zeum 50

food and drink **14–17, 114–19**
  restaurant listings **114–19**
Foreign Cinema **82, 83**
Fort Mason **13, 25, 31, 84–6**
Fort Point **88**
Fraenkel Gallery **51**
French Quarter **50**
further reading **99**

G

Galería de la Raza **83**
Gaslight Cove **85**
gay issues **10, 13, 23, 25, 77, 99**
Geary Street **21, 51**
geography **11**
Ghirardelli's **32**
Ginsberg, Allen **10, 25, 38**
gold **10, 24**
Golden Gate Bridge **10, 11, 22,
  88, 89**
Golden Gate Fortune Cookie
  Factory **44, 45**
Golden Gate National Recre-
  ational Area (GGNRA) **84**
Golden Gate Park **10, 13, 20,
  25, 70–4**
  California Academy
    of Sciences **71–2**
  Conservatory of Flowers **72, 74**
  de Young Museum **13, 25, 70**
  Garden of Shakespeare's
    Flowers **72**
  Japanese Tea Garden **71**
  Koret Children's Quarter **73**
  McLaren, John (statue) **73**
  National Aids Memorial
    Grove **73**
  San Francisco Botanical
    Garden **72–3**
Golden Gate Promenade **87–9**
Grace Cathedral **25, 60–1**
Grant Avenue **37, 41, 42–3**
Grant House **67**
Grateful Dead **20, 25**
Great American Music Hall **20**
green issues **13, 104**
Greenwich Steps **40**

H

Haas-Lilienthaal House **66–7**
Haight-Ashbury **10, 11, 13, 18,
  19, 25, 70, 74–5**
Hammond Hall, William **24**
Harvey Milk Plaza **77**
Hayes Valley **19, 53–7**
health **13, 100**
history **24–5**
Holiday, Billie **25**
hotel listings **108–113**
Hungry I **38**
Huntingdon Park **60**
Hyde Street **63**
Hyde Street Pier **31**
  Historic Ships Collection **31**

I

Ina Coolbrith Park **61**
insurance **100**
internet **100**
Intercontinental Hotel **59**

J

Jackson Square **18, 36**
James Leary Flood Mansion **67**
Japan Center **19**
Japantown **19, 64–5, 69**
jazz **20, 123**
Jefferson Street **29–30**

K

Kerouac, Jack **10, 38**

L

Lafayette Park **65**
Levi's Plaza **40**
Levi Strauss **40**
Lincoln Park **11**
Lombard Street **62, 63**
Louise M. Davies Symphony
  Hall **57, 121**
Lucas, George **22**

M

1360 Montgomery **40**
McClure, Michael **10**
McQueen, Steve **22**
Magic Theater **21, 84, 85, 123**
Maiden Lane **51**
Maltese Falcon, The **22, 23**
Marin Headlands **84**
Marina **11, 21, 24, 84–6**
Marina Green **85**
markets **19**
media **100–1**
Milk, Harvey **25**
Mingus, Charles **20, 25**
Mission District **11, 16, 18, 19,
  21, 25, 79–83**
Mission Dolores **10, 22, 79,
  80, 81**
Mission Dolores Park **81**
money **101, 102, 103**
movies **21, 22–3, 80–3, 123**
Muir Woods **84**
Municipal Pier **31**
Musée Mécanique **30**
Museo Italo-Americano **84–5**
Museum of the African
  Diaspora (MoAD) **48**
Museum of Craft and
  Folk Art **51**
music **20, 56–7, 121, 122, 123**

N

Napier Lane **40**
Newsome, Gavin **10, 25**
nightlife **13, 21, 79, 81, 120–3**
Nob Hill **11, 25, 58–63**
North Beach **10, 11, 16, 19, 20,
  21, 22, 36–40**
North Beach Museum **39**

O

Octagon House **68–9**
Old St Mary's Church **43**
Old Vedanta Society Temple **68**
opening times **18, 102**